THE COMPLETE PIANO PLAYER
OMNIBUS EDITION

Exclusive Distributors:
Music Sales Corporation
257 Park Avenue South, New York, NY 10010, USA

This book Copyright © 1984 and 1985 by
Amsco Publications
Order No. AM 39645
International Standard Book Number: 0.8256.2439.8

Designed by Howard Brown
Photography by Peter Wood
Arranged by Kenneth Baker

Printed in the United States of America by
Vicks Lithograph and Printing Corporation

THE COMPLETE PIANO PLAYER
OMNIBUS EDITION
BOOKS 1, 2, 3, 4 and 5
by Kenneth Baker

Amsco Publications
New York/London/Sydney

BOOK 1

BOOK 2

BOOK 3

BOOK 4

BOOK 5

THE COMPLETE PIANO PLAYER
BOOK 1

'By the end of this book you will
be reading music and playing
twenty four popular songs, including
*Love Me Tender, This Ole House,
Annie's Song,* and *Singin' In The Rain.*'

Kenneth Baker

Amsco Publications
New York/London/Sydney

Exclusive Distributors:
Music Sales Corporation
257 Park Avenue South, New York, NY 10010, USA

This book Copyright © 1984 and 1985 by
Amsco Publications
Order No. AM 39645
International Standard Book Number: 0.8256.2439.8

Designed by Howard Brown
Photography by Peter Wood
Arranged by Kenneth Baker

Printed in the United States of America by
Vicks Lithograph and Printing Corporation

CONTENTS

ABOUT THIS BOOK

This is the first book in an exciting new piano course called The Complete Piano Player.

Right from the start of the course, you play songs made famous by artists like The Beatles...Ralph McTell and Abba. Many of the songs are tunes you've often heard. And because these tunes are familiar to you, you can tell right away when you're playing them correctly.

This step-by-step course teaches you to play popular music and tuneful, light classics the right way. You learn to read music in easy stages, and by the end of the course you will be able to tackle almost any song from sheet music.

Even if you are learning on your own, you can still become an accomplished pianist with the help of The Complete Piano Player. This is because the text is easy to follow, and backed with illustrations and diagrams. Each illustration and diagram is clearly explained. They have been designed to train your fingers to reach for the right keys, to make pleasing sounds, and play expressively.

A special feature of this book is the Keyboard Guide. With its help you can locate and learn the notes of the piano with no trouble at all.

Just one word of advice. Try to play regularly every day. Even a short period of daily playing will help you become The Complete Piano Player.

TO TEACHERS

You will find The Complete Piano Player just the course you need for today's students. It teaches sound techniques from the beginning. And it is based on music which will keep your students interested throughout.

HOW TO SIT CORRECTLY

It is important to sit correctly at the piano. The more comfortable you are, the easier it is to play. Sit as shown here and you will always feel comfortable and relaxed.

Sit facing the middle of the instrument, your feet opposite the pedals. Sit upright. Adjust your seat so that your arms are level with the keyboard–or sloping down slightly towards it.

POSITION OF THE HANDS

Support your hands from the wrists. Curve your fingers slightly as if you were grasping lightly an imaginary ball.

With the tips of your fingers cover five adjacent notes in each hand. This is the normal Five-Finger Playing Position. It is also the hand's most relaxed state. After all fingering and hand changes during a piece, you should return to this position.

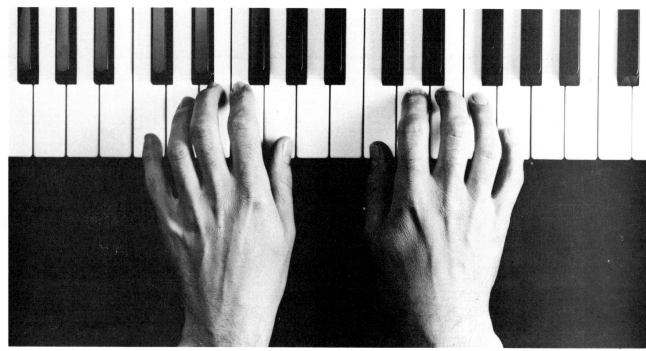

THE PIANO KEYBOARD

2

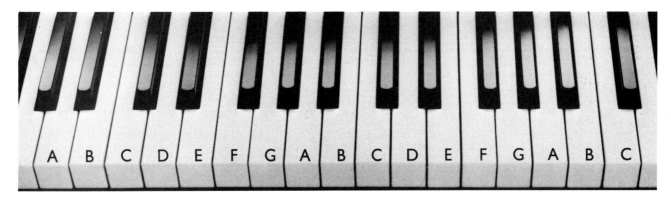

There are only seven letter names used in music: A B C D E F G.
These seven letter names repeat over and over again on the keyboard.

The black keys are arranged in groups of twos and threes.

HOW TO LEARN THE WHITE KEYS: C, D & E

Use the black keys to locate the white keys.
For example, 'D' lies between two black keys.

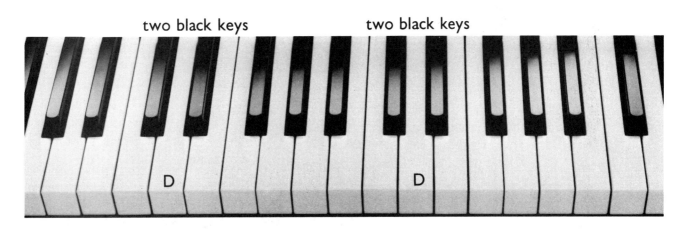

To the left of D lies C.
To the right of D lies E:

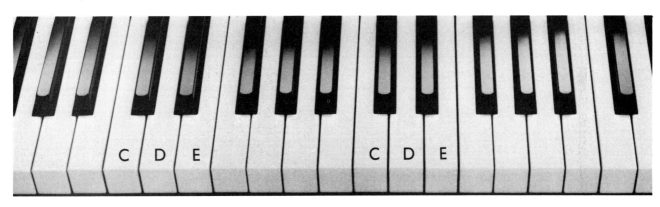

HOW TO LEARN THE WHITE KEYS: F, G, A & B

Use the groups of three black keys to locate F, G, A and B (the remaining four letters of the musical alphabet):

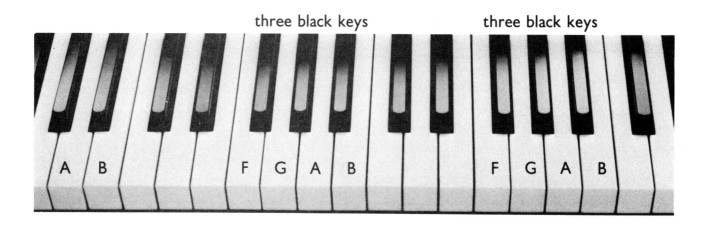

Find all the F's, G's, A's and B's on your piano.
Play each note in turn and name it.

HOW TO LEARN THE WHITE KEYS: C to B

Play every 'set' of white notes, beginning with C and ending on B. Play in all positions on the piano. Do this several times, naming the notes as you play them.

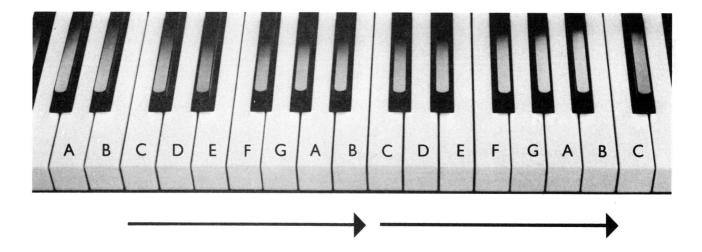

You now know all the white notes and their names.

AN IMPORTANT NOTE: MIDDLE C

3

One of the most important notes on the piano is Middle C. This is the C nearest the middle of the instrument, directly opposite the manufacturer's name, as you sit at the piano.

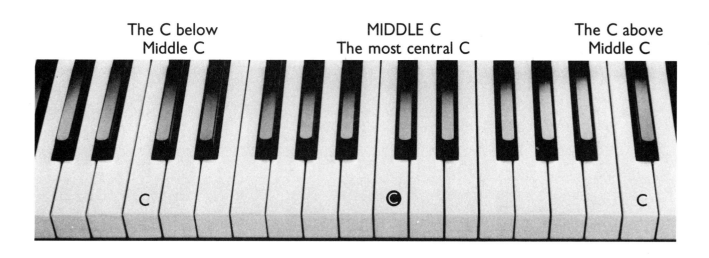

The C below Middle C

MIDDLE C The most central C

The C above Middle C

Look at the illustration above. From it, you will see that:

The C to the left of Middle C is called 'The C below middle C.'

The C to the right of middle C is called 'The C above middle C.' You should, at this stage, be able to find these three C's right away. Learn to find them this easy way:

● Play Middle C with the right hand (any finger will do).
● Play Middle C with the left hand.
● Play The C below Middle C with the left hand.
● Play The C above Middle C with the right hand.
● Finally: play Middle C again with one of the fingers of each hand.

You now know where to find Middle C and the C's immediately above and below it.

FINGER NUMBERS

4

To make learning easy, the fingers of both hands are given numbers:

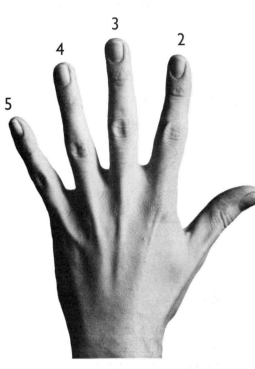

left hand

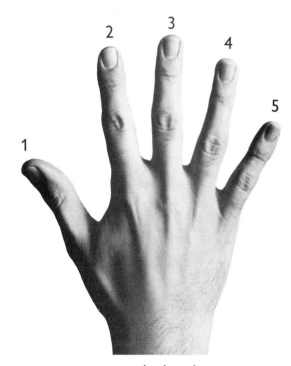

right hand

You will see that the thumb counts as finger Number 1.

To familiarize you with the finger numbers of the right hand, we are going to play the great jazz number: *When The Saints Go Marching In.*

Before you start to play, cover the five notes from Middle C to G above it with the five fingers of your right hand, like this:

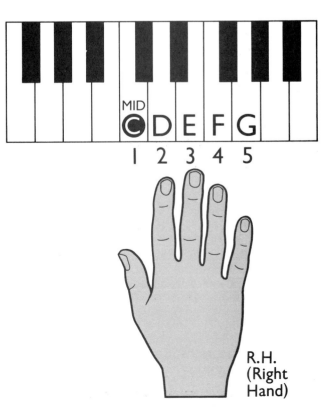

Now play each note with the fingers shown below. To help you play in time, tap your foot to the music. The little diagrams below the finger numbers ❗ show you when to tap.

Notice that every so often the tune 'stays still,' while you go on tapping your foot. Remember to hold the note down during this time.

WHEN THE SAINTS GO MARCHING IN
Traditional

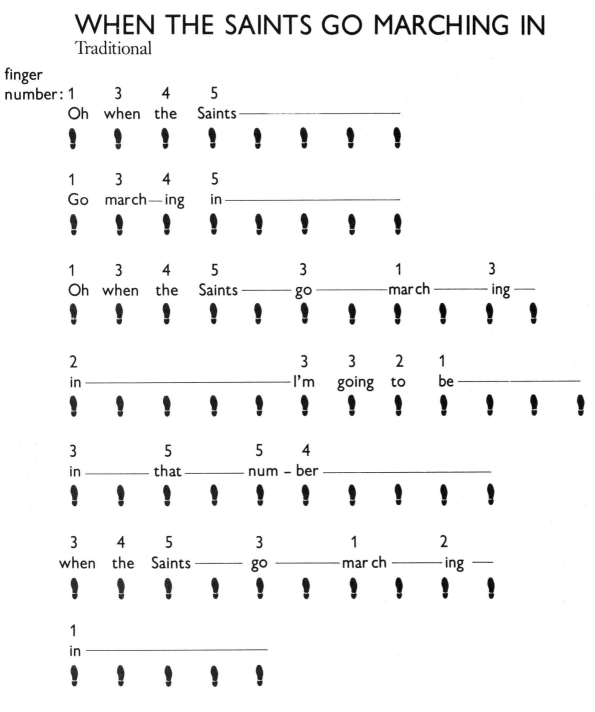

You now know the finger numbers of the right hand.

HOW TO PLAY LEGATO

5

Legato means 'joined up'. When you play legato, your playing sounds smooth and connected.

To get this smooth and connected effect, as each new note is played you release the preceding note. In other words: one finger exactly replaces another. The result is a continuous, unbroken flow of sound. This is true legato playing.

Always play legato unless the music is marked otherwise.

In your efforts to play legato, never let one sound overlap the next. If you do, you may get an ugly sound mixture. Your ear will tell you when you are playing legato. Remember:

● No gaps.
● No overlaps.

Now play *When The Saints Go Marching In* again. Are you playing smoothly? Do all the notes join up? If so, you are playing legato.

LEFT HAND FINGER NUMBERS

You are now going to learn the left hand finger numbers by playing the traditional tune: *Banks Of The Ohio.*

Before you start to play, cover the five notes from C below Middle C to G with the five fingers of your left hand:

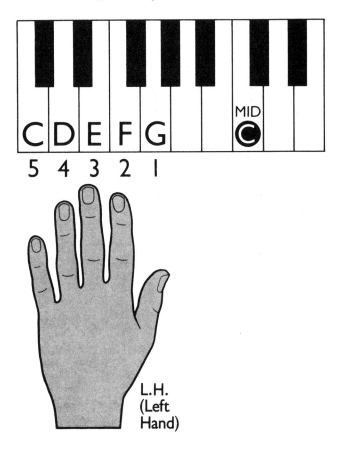

Now, play each note according to the finger numbers given.

Tap your foot to keep time, as before…

Remember: play legato

BANKS OF THE OHIO
Traditional

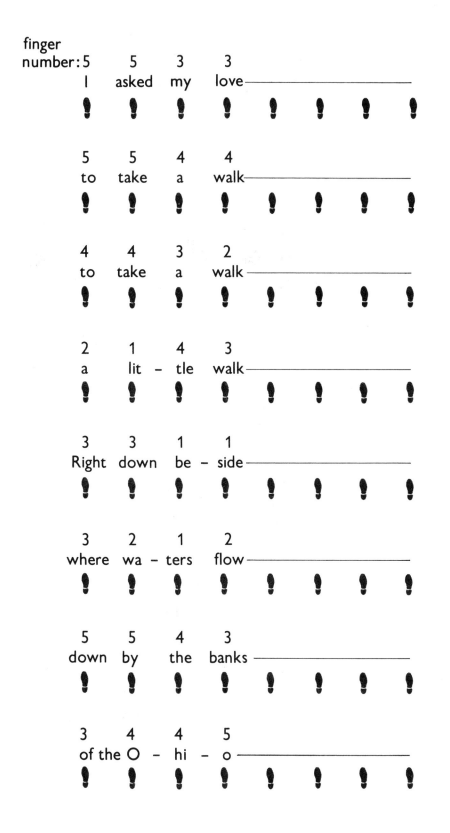

You now know the finger numbers of the left hand.

HOW NOTES ARE WRITTEN

6

Musical notes are written on groups of
five lines called 'staves':

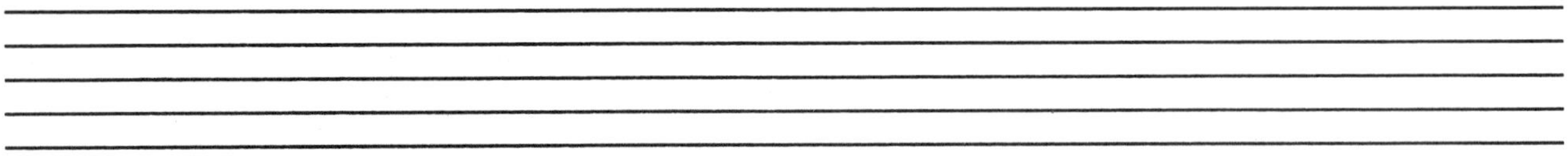

A staff

The notes may be written on any 'line':

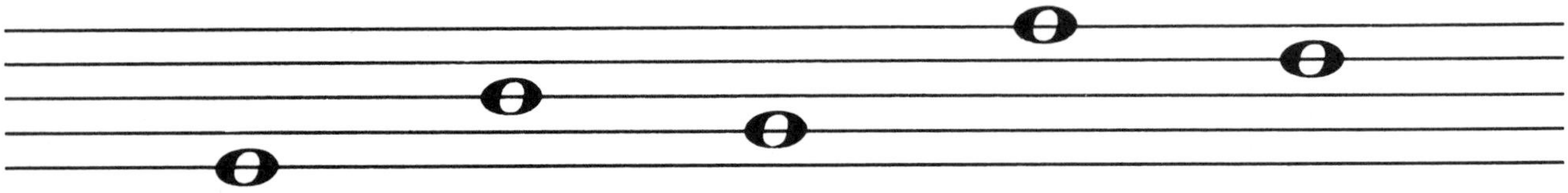

or in any 'space' between lines:

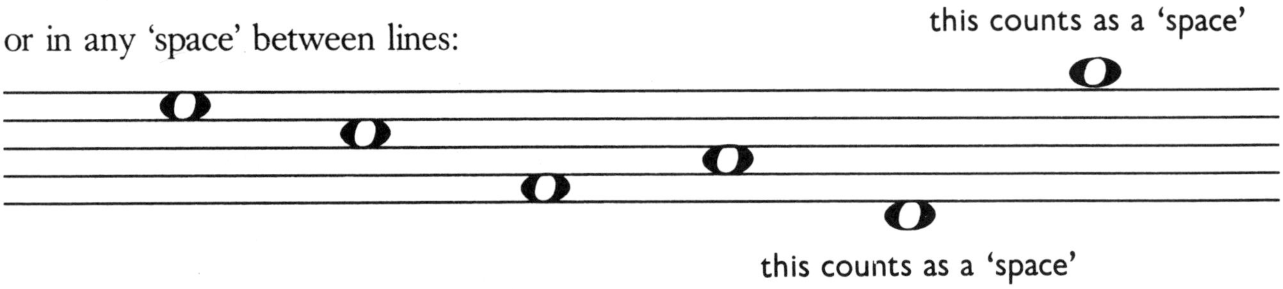

this counts as a 'space'

this counts as a 'space'

The piano needs two staves: one for the
top half of the instrument:

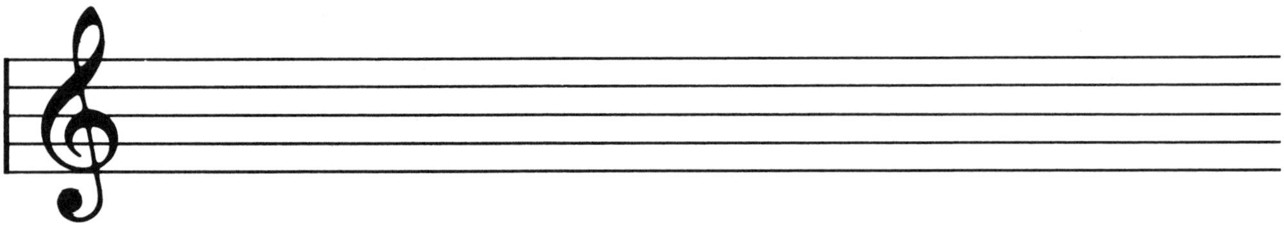

This sign is called the 'Treble Clef'

and one for the bottom half:

This sign is called the 'Bass Clef'

The two staves are joined together by a 'brace':

Brace

The notes on the upper staff (indicated by the Treble Clef) are usually played by the right hand.

The notes on the lower staff (indicated by the Bass Clef) are usually played by the left hand.

Middle C falls on a line exactly between the two staves.

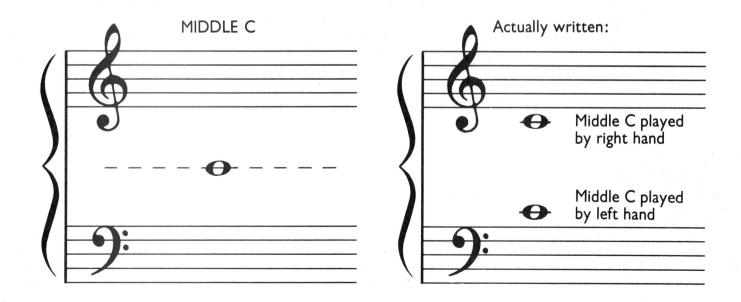

MIDDLE C

Actually written:

Middle C played by right hand

Middle C played by left hand

The Middle C line is never drawn in its entirety since that would cause confusion with the other lines. A partial line is all that is needed:

Cover the five notes Middle C to G with the fingers of your right hand:

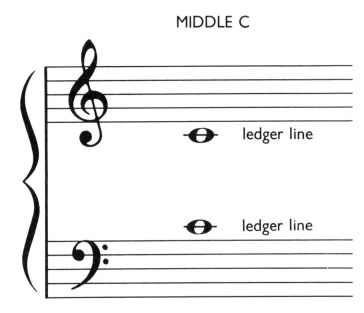

MIDDLE C

ledger line

ledger line

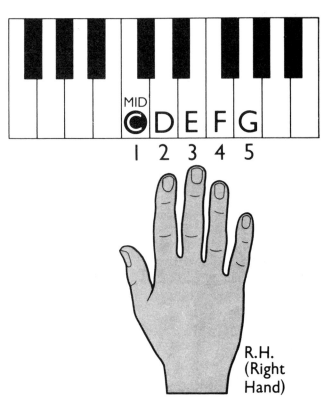

R.H.
(Right
Hand)

Such partial lines are called 'ledger lines.'

Now let's see how your first five notes for right hand are written:

You used these notes in *When The Saints Go Marching In,* on page 11.

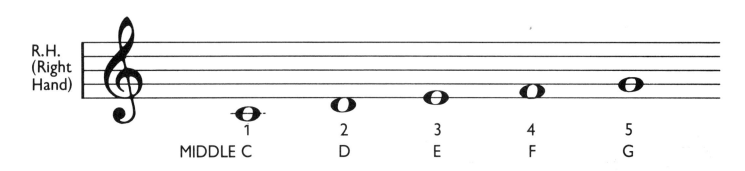

R.H.
(Right
Hand)

| 1 | 2 | 3 | 4 | 5 |
| MIDDLE C | D | E | F | G |

Learn these notes now.

Cover the five notes with the correct fingers of your right hand and play the next tune: *I Know Where I'm Going:*

I KNOW WHERE I'M GOING

Words & Music: Herbert Hughes

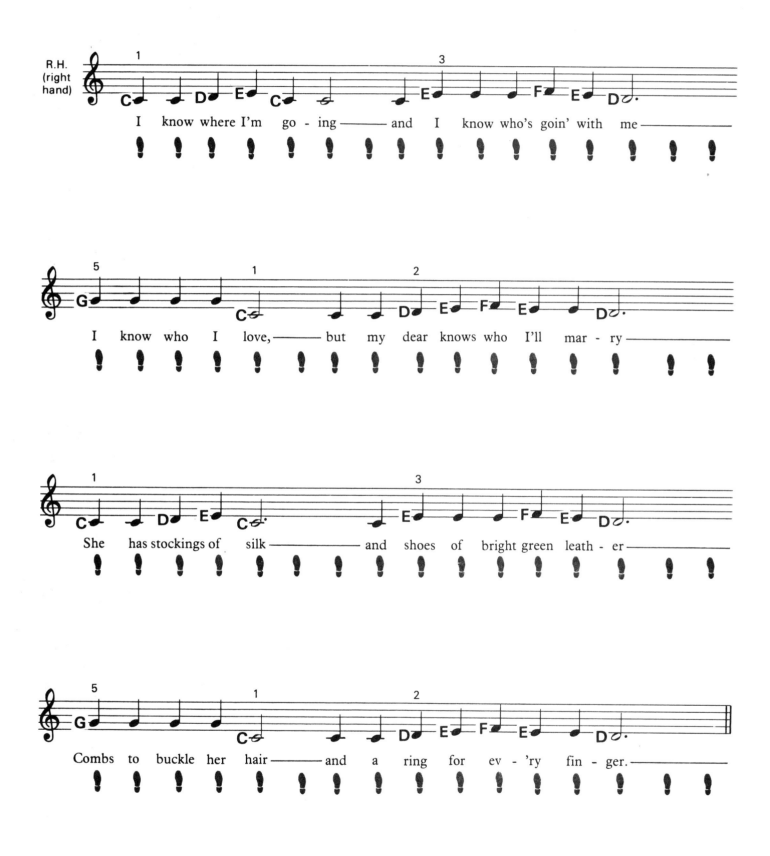

7

You now know your first five right hand notes and how they are written.

Let's learn the first five left hand notes. Start at Middle C and work down the keyboard (i.e. to the left).
These are the five notes:

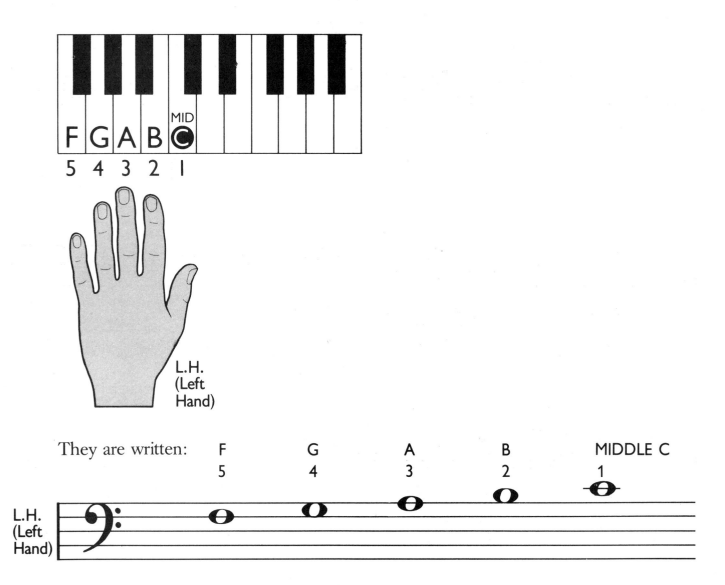

They are written:

F	G	A	B	MIDDLE C
5	4	3	2	1

Learn these notes now.

Cover the notes with the correct fingers of your left hand and play your next tune:
Rivers Of Babylon.

RIVERS OF BABYLON

Words & Music adapted by Brent Dowe and Trevor McMaughton.

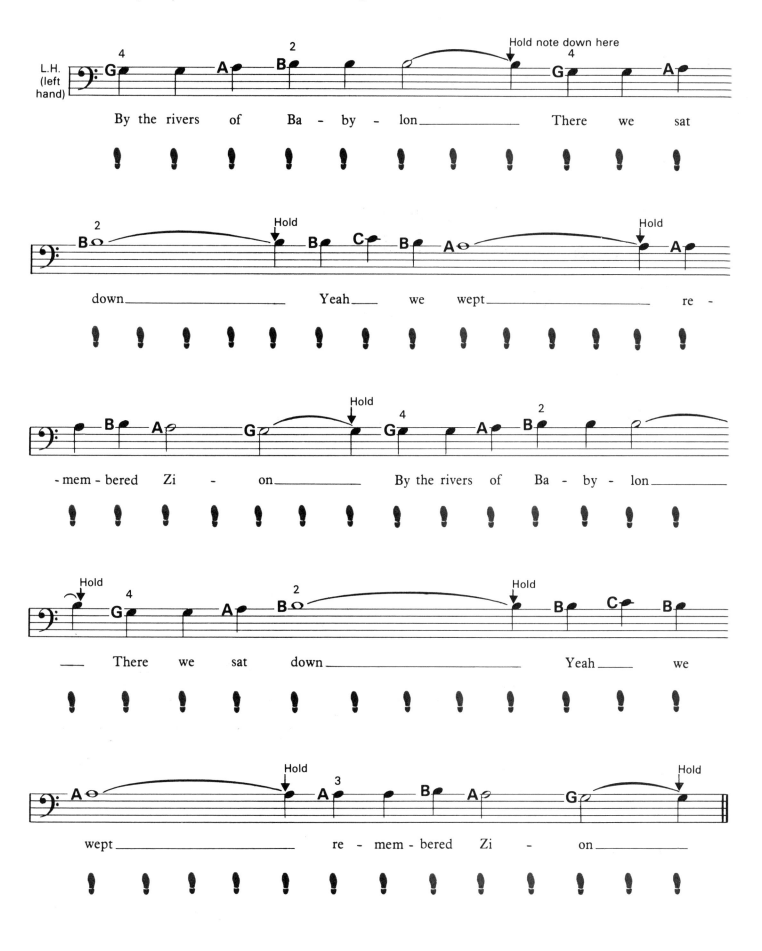

You now know nine important notes
and how they are written:

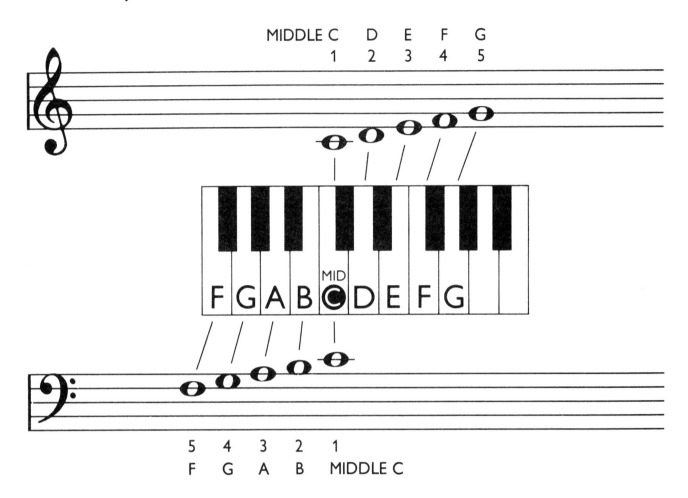

These nine notes are all that are needed
to play all the songs in this book.

After this, new notes will be added
gradually. Keyboard charts will be given
to illustrate new notes as they occur.

The cardboard chart included with this
book fits over the piano keyboard and
may be used for reference. In addition, in
this book, 'letter names' have been
written against the notes. **But, you
should memorize all new notes as
soon as possible.**

MUSICAL TIMING AND THE BEAT

8

The 'Beat' is the name given to the rhythmic pulse felt behind most music.

When you were tapping your foot to *When The Saints Go Marching In, Banks Of The Ohio,* and *Rivers Of Babylon,* you were tapping out the beat. In most tunes there is a series of natural 'accents', which recur regularly every few beats. A line called a 'bar line' is drawn in front of every one of these natural accents. These lines divide the music into 'bars' or 'measures'.

In the above example the beat is written in 'quarter notes':

(Note that the 'tails' or 'stems' may be written up or down).

Look at the above example again, and you will see that there are four quarter notes to the bar. This is indicated at the beginning of the piece like this:

The above pair of numbers is called the 'time signature'. In every time signature there is:

An 'upper figure': this shows how many beats there are in the bar (four in our example).

A 'lower figure': this shows how the beats are written. In our example the lower figure 4 means that the beats are written as quarter notes.

Here is another example:

This time, the upper figure tells you that there are three beats to the bar. The lower figure is still 4, so there are: Three quarter notes to the bar.

The next song you are going to learn is *This Ole House*. It is written entirely in quarter notes:

Tap your foot on each quarter note – this will help keep you in time.

You will be using the same five right hand notes as before:

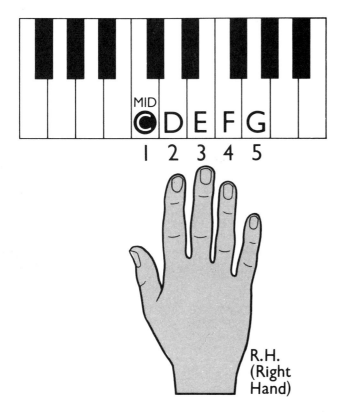

Cover these notes before you start to play. Your first note is E, played by the 3rd finger.

Notice that there are four quarter notes in each bar, and the tune starts on the third beat of the bar.

THIS OLE HOUSE

Words & Music by: Stuart Hamblen

start playing here

This ole house once knew his child – ren, this ole house once knew his wife___ This ole house was home and com – fort as they fought the storms of life___ This ole house once rang with laugh – ter, this ole house heard ma – ny shouts___ Now he trem – bles in the dark – ness when the light – nin' walks a – bout.___

2 beats only
in this bar
(making good
the deficiency
in bar 1).

You now know about quarter notes.

DEVELOPING YOUR SENSE OF RHYTHM

9

The melody notes of *This Ole House* corresponded with the quarter note beat exactly. But usually a melody includes a number of notes of longer duration.

This is how some of these longer time notes are written:

Name of note	How written					Duration
Half Note	𝅗𝅥	=	♩	♩		Lasts for two quarter note beats
Dotted Half Note	𝅗𝅥.	=	♩	♩	♩	Lasts for three quarter note beats
Whole Note	𝅝	=	♩	♩	♩ ♩	Lasts for four quarter note beats

To get you used to these different time notes, I want you to play now some rhythm exercises. They are written entirely on Middle C.

The first rhythm exercise is for the right hand. It features quarter notes, half notes, dotted half notes and whole notes. In each bar, there are four quarter notes (or their equivalent).
Choose a suitable speed (not too fast), and maintain the same speed throughout. Tap your foot once on every quarter note beat.

RHYTHM EXERCISE 1

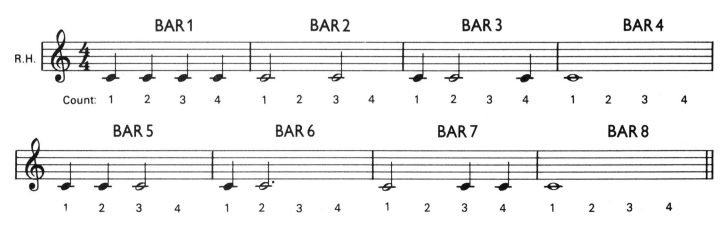

Bar 1   Play Middle C on beats 1, 2, 3 and 4.

Bar 2   Play C on beat 1 and let the sound continue while you count and tap beat 2. Play C on beat 3 and let the sound continue while you count and tap beat 4.

Bar 3   Play C on beat 1.
Play C on beat 2 and let the sound continue while you count and tap beat 3.
Play C on beat 4.

Bar 4   Play C on beat 1 and let the sound continue while you count and tap beats 2, 3 and 4.

Continue similarly to bar 8.

Did you keep your speed constant?

Now another rhythm exercise, this time for the left hand. Again you will be using Middle C only.

This exercise is in $\frac{3}{4}$ Time, in other words there are three quarter notes (or their equivalent) to the bar.

RHYTHM EXERCISE 2

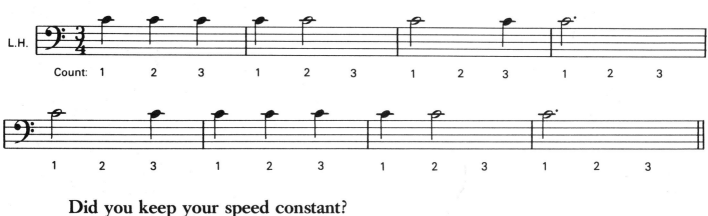

Did you keep your speed constant?

You now know about:
1 beat notes ♩ Quarter notes
2 beat notes ♩ Half notes

3 beat notes ♩. Dotted half notes
4 beat notes 𝅝 Whole notes

25

MORE ABOUT RHYTHM

10

From now on you will be called upon to put your knowledge of rhythm to work. The popular tunes you are going to learn will use all four kinds of notes: quarter notes, half notes, dotted half notes and whole notes. Check that you know them thoroughly.

You are first going to play *White Rose Of Athens* for the right hand. As usual before you start to play, cover the notes Middle C to G with the five fingers of your right hand.

The tune starts on Middle C played with the thumb. There are four quarter notes (or their equivalent) to the bar.

Remember to play legato

WHITE ROSE OF ATHENS

Music: Manos Hadjidakis. Words: Norman Newell.
Additional Words: Archie Bleyer.

Now two famous Beatles themes, both for left hand. Before you start to play, cover the notes Middle C to F with the fingers of your left hand.

The first theme starts on F with the fifth finger and you start playing on the second beat of the bar.

Remember to play legato.

CAN'T BUY ME LOVE/ SHE LOVES YOU

Words & Music: John Lennon & Paul McCartney

NOTES REQUIRED

FINGERING 5 4 3 2 1

⟨ LEFT HAND ⟩

Now a Beatles tune for right hand: *Help*.

There are four quarter notes to the bar. You will be using quarter notes, half notes and whole notes.

Before you start to play, cover the notes Middle C to G with the five fingers of your right hand.

The tune starts on the second beat of the bar with the note E (3rd finger).

HELP

Words & Music: John Lennon and Paul McCartney

NOTES REQUIRED

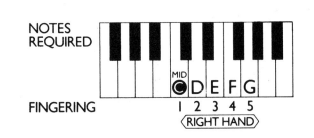

FINGERING

When I was young – er, So much young – er than to — day.

Count: 1 **2** 3 4 1 2 3 4 1 2 3 4 1 2 3 4

Start playing here ↑

Nev – er need – ed an – y – bod – y's help in an – y way.

1 2 3 4 1 2 3 4 1 2 3 4 1 2 3 4

Oh but now those days are gone I'm not so self as — sured_____

1 2 3 4 1 2 3 4 1 2 3 4 1 2 3 4

*This curved line concerns the singer only and is called a 'Melisma Mark' or 'Singer's Slur'. Here the singer continues the syllable '-sured' through the three notes E, D and C. Look on the next page for five more 'Singer's Slurs'.

Now I find I've changed my mind, I've o—pened up the doors.

Help me if you can, I'm feel—ing down_____ And I

do ap—pre—ci—ate you be—ing 'round_____

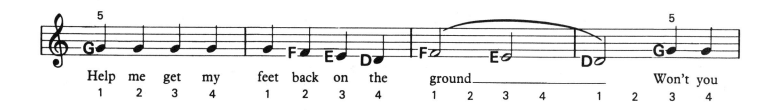

Help me get my feet back on the ground_____ Won't you

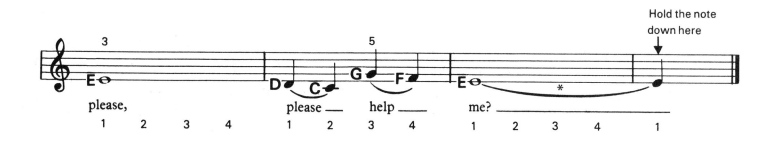

Hold the note down here

please, please ___ help ___ me? _____

*This curved line is a 'tie' (see page 31) not a 'Singer's Slur'.

EXCERPT FROM A FAMOUS CLASSIC

Your next piece is the Largo from *The New World Symphony* by Dvořák.

The first part is played by your left hand; the second part is played by your right hand; the final part is played by your left hand.

Watch out for quarter notes, half notes and whole notes in this piece.

LARGO
(FROM THE NEW WORLD SYMPHONY)

By: Antonin Dvořák

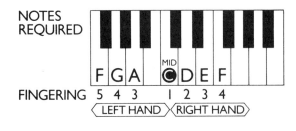

TIES

12

Let me just remind you of the names of the time notes and how long they last:

Quarter note	♩	1 beat
Half note	♪	2 beats
Dotted half note	♪.	3 beats
Whole note	o	4 beats

Each of the time notes may be extended by the use of a 'Tie'. A tie is a curved line connecting two notes of the same pitch – in other words, two notes in the same position on the stave.

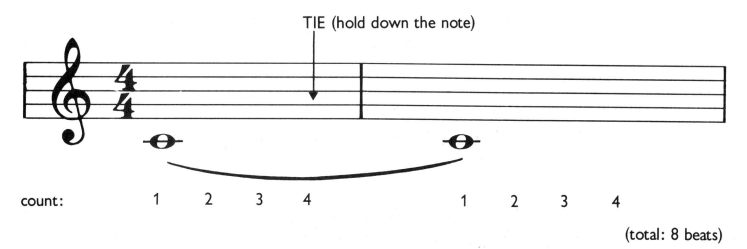

Here you play the first Middle C and count for the second Middle C without striking the note again. Total time: 2 whole notes, or 8 quarter note beats.

A reminder:

You have already met ties in *Rivers Of Babylon, White Rose Of Athens, She Loves You,* and *Help* (see the last note E).

Now play all these pieces through again, and this time pay particular attention to the ties.

TWO MORE POPULAR TUNES WITH TIES

13

The next tune, *Carry That Weight*, also features ties and is for the right hand. Before you start to play, cover the usual notes, Middle C to G, with the right hand fingers.

The tune starts on the second beat of the bar.

CARRY THAT WEIGHT
Words & Music: John Lennon and Paul McCartney.

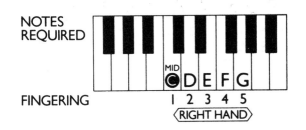

NOTES REQUIRED

FINGERING

Here is another tune which features ties.
It is for the left hand.

Before you start to play, cover Middle C
to F with the five fingers of the left hand:

This tune starts on G with the 4th finger.
There are four quarter notes (or their
equivalent) per bar, and the tune starts
on beat 2:

ONE OF THOSE SONGS
(LE BAL DE MADAME DE MORTEMOUILLE)
English lyric: Will Holt. Music: Gerard Calvi

NOTES
REQUIRED

FINGERING   4 3 2 1
< LEFT HAND >

**Now you know about ties and how
they make the notes last longer.**

PLAYING FROM TWO STAVES

14 This is the first time that you have had to read music written on two staves. In your next piece both hands share the tune. This is why two staves are necessary. Play the piece several times

and get used to reading two staves.

The left hand plays first. It starts on G with the 4th finger.

LOVE ME TENDER
Words and Music: Elvis Presley & Vera Matson

34

TWO STAVES AGAIN

15 You will use both hands again in the next piece: *Mary's Little Boy Child*. The right hand plays first. It starts on E with the 3rd finger.

MARY'S LITTLE BOY CHILD
Words & Music: Jester Hairston

PHRASE MARKS

16

Curved lines over or under the notes are called: 'Phrase Marks,' or 'Slurs.' Phrase marks are not to be confused with 'ties':

Phrase mark (play legato)   **Tie (hold down the note)**

Unless directed otherwise, play all notes within phrase marks legato (joined up).

I'D LIKE TO TEACH THE WORLD TO SING

Words & Music: Roger Cook, Roger Greenaway, Billy Backer & Billy Davis

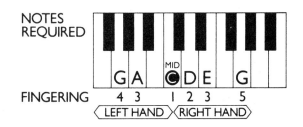

NOTES REQUIRED

G A MID C D E G

FINGERING 4 3 1 2 3 5

〈LEFT HAND〉 〈RIGHT HAND〉

Count: 1 2 3 4   1 2 3 4   1 2 3 4   1 2 3 4   1 2 3 4

Start playing here ↑

STREETS OF LONDON

Words & Music: Ralph McTell

EIGHTH NOTES

17

The next three pieces feature a new time note: the eighth note.

Eighth notes

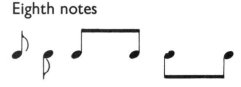

Eighth notes move twice as fast as the basic quarter note beat:

If you say the word 'and' between beat numbers, it will give you the time of the eighth note. You will come across eighth notes in bars 10 and 11 of the famous theme from the *Choral Symphony* by Beethoven. In this and the following two pieces I have marked the places at which you should say 'and' when counting.

Theme from CHORAL SYMPHONY

By: Ludwig van Beethoven

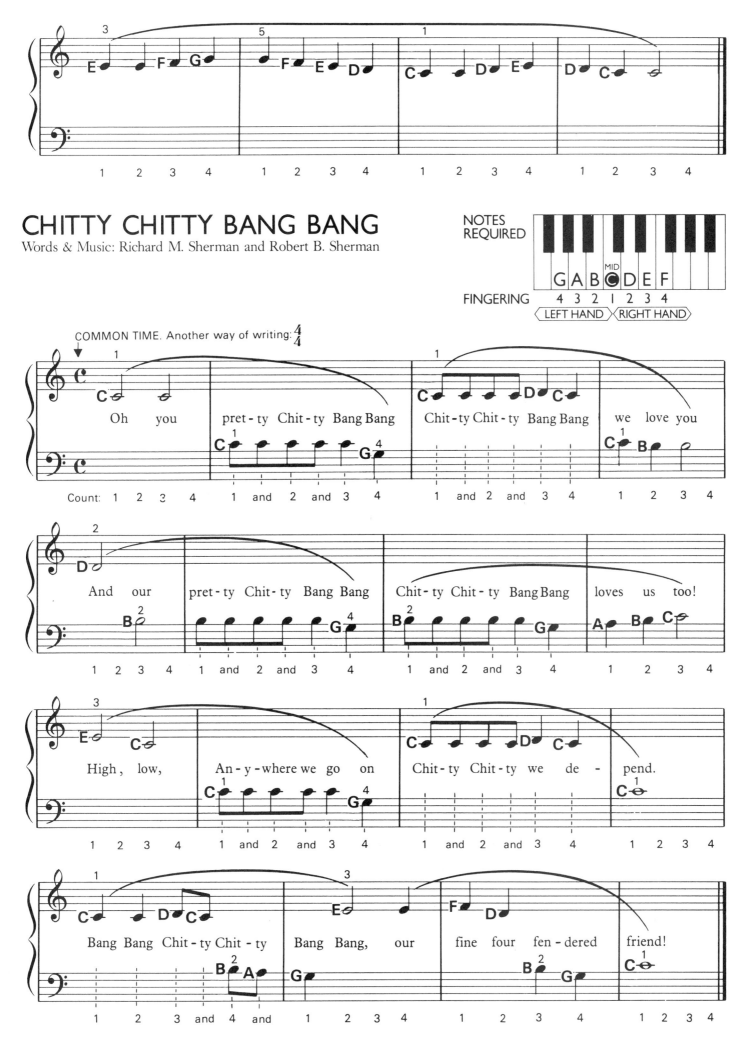

CHITTY CHITTY BANG BANG

Words & Music: Richard M. Sherman and Robert B. Sherman

STACCATO AND ACCENT

18

A dot over or under a note means that the note is to be played 'Staccato,' which means 'cut short.' Keep the wrist loose and 'peck' at the note with the finger. Staccato (cut short) is the opposite of legato (smooth and connected).

Staccato – cut the note(s) short

A dash over or under a note means hold the note for its full value, or even a fraction more.

Accent (Tenuto mark) – hold the note(s) for its full value

In the next piece make the contrast between staccato and accented notes.

OLD MACDONALD HAD A FARM
Traditional

NOTES REQUIRED

G A | MID C | D E
FINGERING 4 3 | 1 2 3
⟨LEFT HAND⟩⟨RIGHT HAND⟩

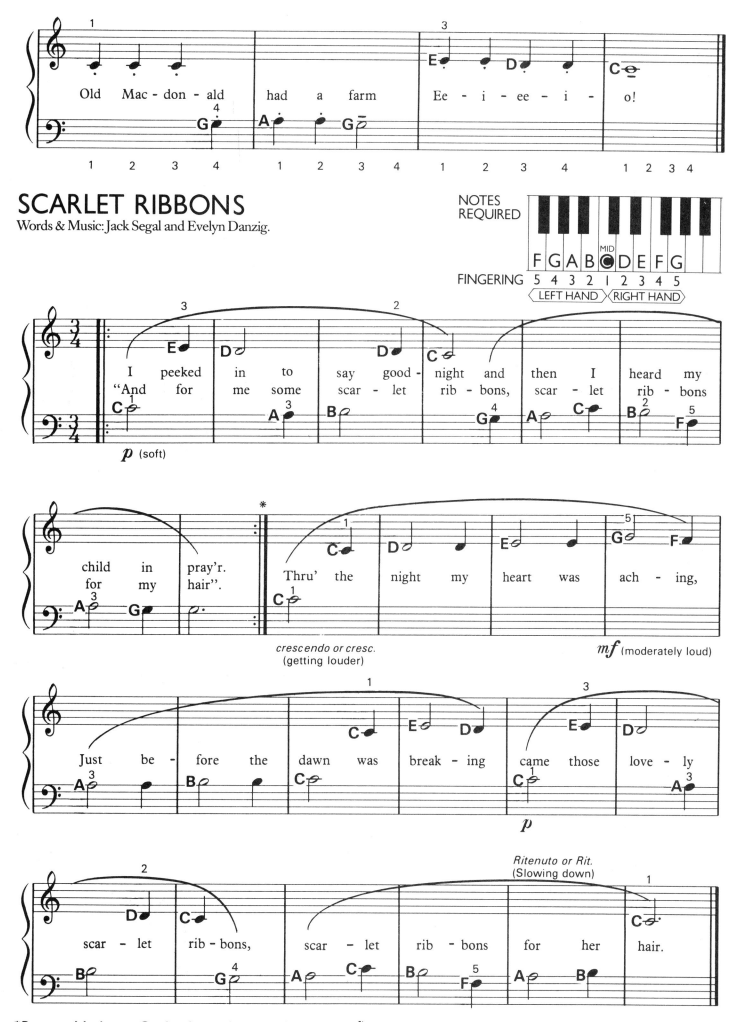

SCARLET RIBBONS
Words & Music: Jack Segal and Evelyn Danzig.

*Repeat Marking. Go back to the matching sign: ‖: and play through the first 8 Bars again.

RESTS AND SILENCE

19 Silence in music is important. Silences can be dramatic, romantic, or add an air of expectancy. To indicate silence in music, signs called 'Rests' are used. Each Time Note has its own rest.

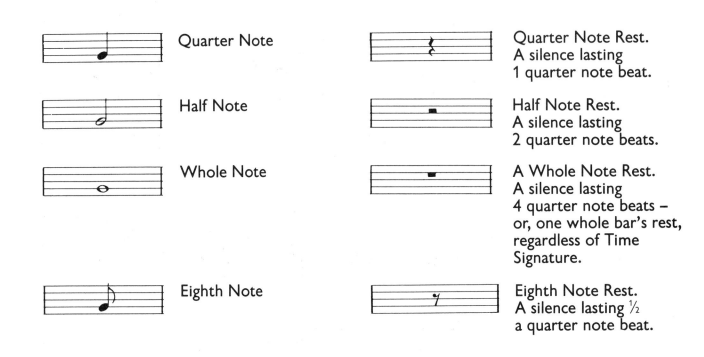

Quarter Note — Quarter Note Rest. A silence lasting 1 quarter note beat.

Half Note — Half Note Rest. A silence lasting 2 quarter note beats.

Whole Note — A Whole Note Rest. A silence lasting 4 quarter note beats – or, one whole bar's rest, regardless of Time Signature.

Eighth Note — Eighth Note Rest. A silence lasting ½ a quarter note beat.

You will come across various rests in *Annie's Song* which you are going to play now. Make sure you respect these silences. The first few rests are 'arrowed' to make it easier for you.

ANNIE'S SONG
Words & Music by John Denver

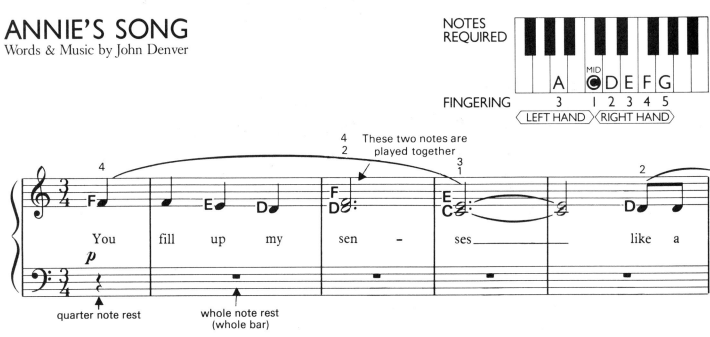

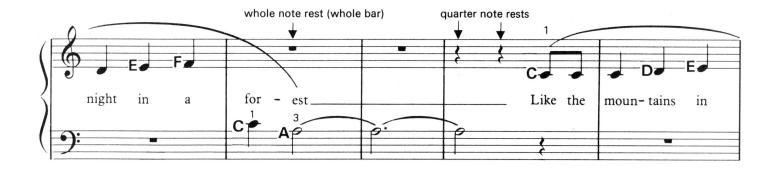

night in a for-est ___ Like the moun-tains in

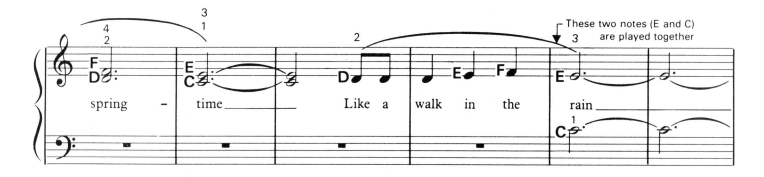

spring-time ___ Like a walk in the rain ___

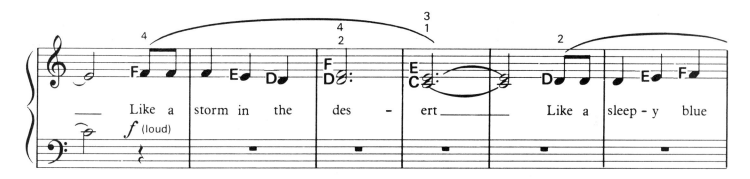

___ Like a storm in the des-ert ___ Like a sleep-y blue

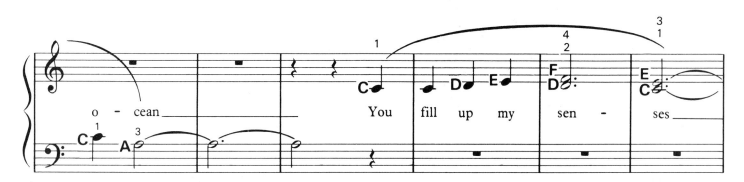

o-cean ___ You fill up my sen - ses ___

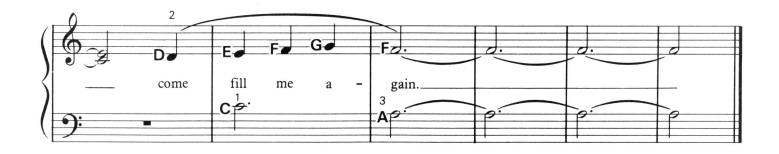

___ come fill me a-gain. ___

I have 'arrowed' the first few rests in this
piece. After that I leave it to you to
watch for and respect the rests.

STRANGERS IN THE NIGHT
Music: Bert Kaempfert. Words: Charles Singleton & Eddie Snyder.

two lone - ly peo - ple we were stran - gers in the night

— up to the mo-ment when we said our first hel - lo, lit - tle did we know,

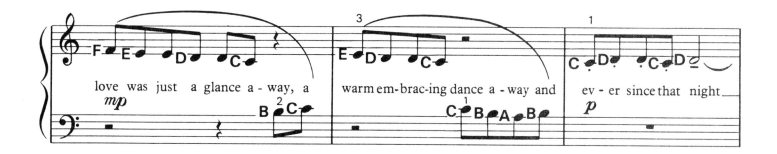

love was just a glance a - way, a warm em-brac-ing dance a - way and ev - er since that night

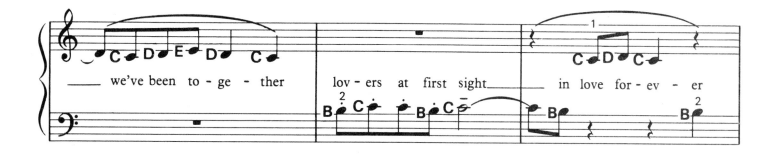

— we've been to - ge - ther lov - ers at first sight in love for - ev - er

It turned out so right for stran - gers in the night.

SINGIN' IN THE RAIN

Words: Arthur Freed. Music: Nacio Herb Brown

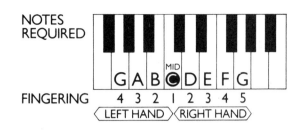

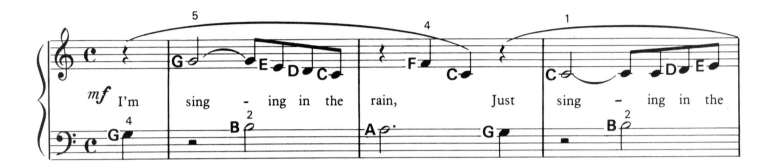

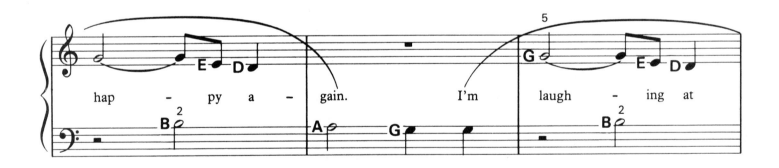

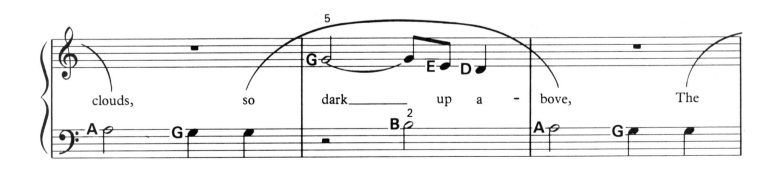

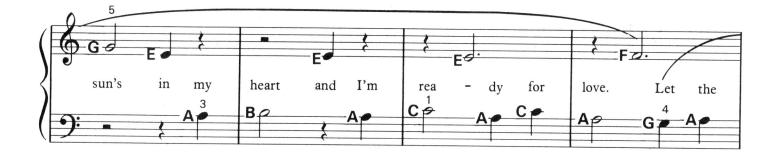

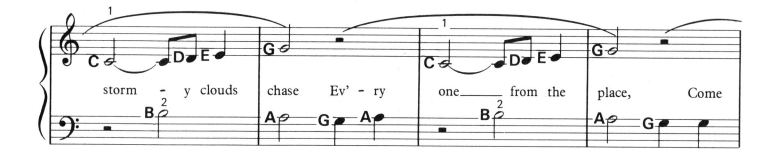

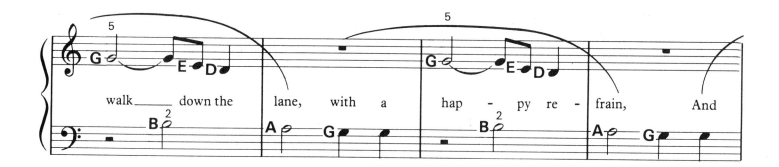

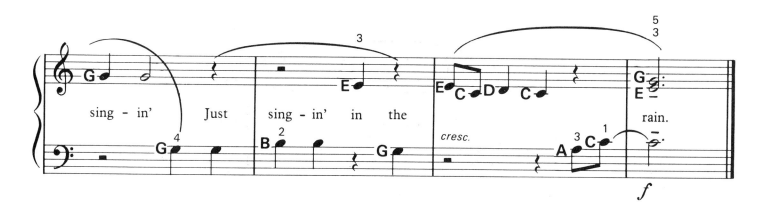

LAST WORD

Congratulations on completing Book One of 'The Complete Piano Player.'

In Book Two you will be:
- Learning new notes
- Finding out more about 'fingering'
- Using sharps and flats
- Understanding something about 'keys'
- Discovering new piano techniques.

In the meantime your last song in this book is: *Super Trouper*

SUPER TROUPER
Words & Music by Benny Andersson and Bjorn Ulvaeus

THE COMPLETE PIANO PLAYER
BOOK 2

'By the end of this book, you will know more about music and you will be playing twenty-two popular songs, including *Bright Eyes, Edelweiss, Hard Day's Night* and *Sailing*.'

Kenneth Baker

Amsco Publications
New York/London/Sydney

Exclusive Distributors:
Music Sales Corporation
257 Park Avenue South, New York, NY 10010, USA

This book Copyright © 1984 and 1985 by
Amsco Publications
Order No. AM 39645
International Standard Book Number: 0.8256.2439.8

Designed by Howard Brown
Photography by Peter Wood
Arranged by Kenneth Baker

Printed in the United States of America by
Vicks Lithograph and Printing Corporation

CONTENTS

ABOUT THIS BOOK

This is the second book in The Complete Piano Player course. You will find it as rewarding to work through as Book 1.

As in the first book, you will learn how to play songs by Elvis Presley...Rod Stewart...The Beatles, and other famous artists and groups. And you will learn famous classics which are a pleasure to play and to listen to.

Carefully follow the lessons, and by the end of the book you will find that you have made excellent progress in reading music and in technique. You will be delighted, too, to find that you have built up a fine repertoire. In all this, you are helped by the easy to follow text combined with numerous, clear diagrams. These are of special value to you if you are working on your own.

Remember to play regularly every day, if only for a short time. Little and often is an excellent way of making rapid progress towards becoming the complete piano player.

TO TEACHERS

The Complete Piano Player course is ideal for teaching today's students. It teaches sound technique from the beginning. At the same time, it is based on music which will keep your students interested throughout the entire course.

NEW NOTES

You start this book by learning these new notes:

A, B, C right hand
E left hand

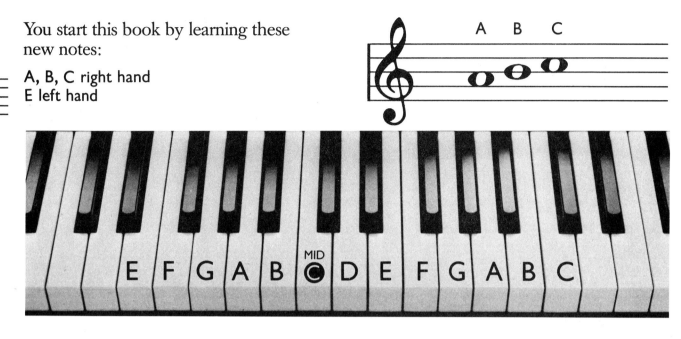

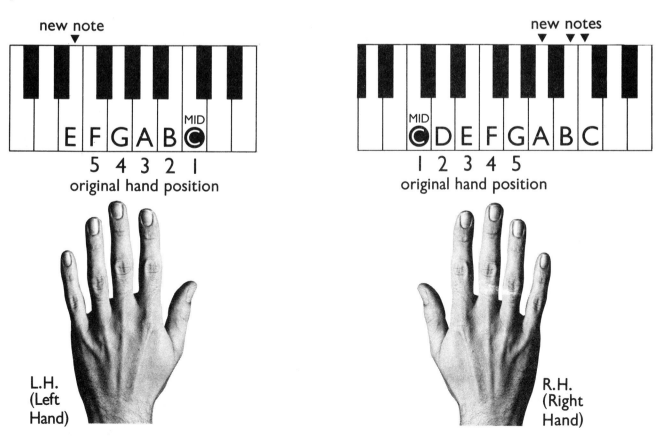

HOW TO FINGER THE NEW NOTES

The new notes illustrated above are beyond the range of your original five-fingered hand positions:

When a single new note is required,
extend your hand to play it, then return
to your original five finger hand position:

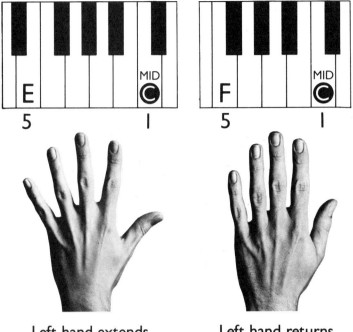

Left hand extends
to play note E

Left hand returns
to original five-finger
position.

When several new notes are to be played
consecutively take up a new five-finger
position covering the new notes:

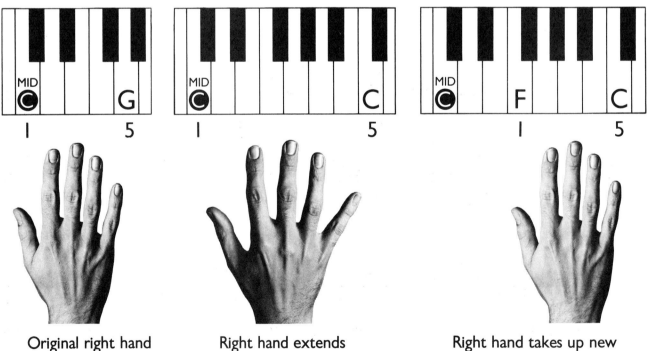

Original right hand
position

Right hand extends

Right hand takes up new
five finger position

I have indicated examples of both the
above situations in the three pieces which
follow: *Sailing, My Own True Love,*
and *Wooden Heart.*

**Note: From now on letter names will
appear alongside new notes only.**

SAILING

Words & Music: Gavin Sutherland

Remember: watch out for changes of hand positions in this and the next two pieces.

MY OWN TRUE LOVE
(TARA'S THEME)
Words: Mack David. Music: Max Steiner.

Always change hand positions smoothly

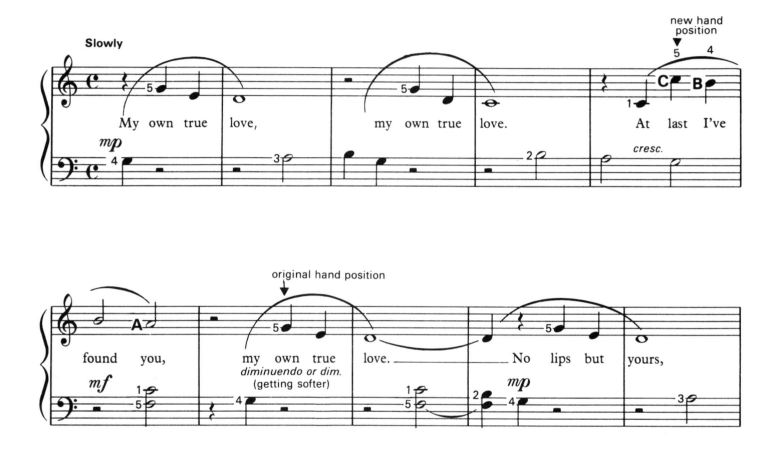

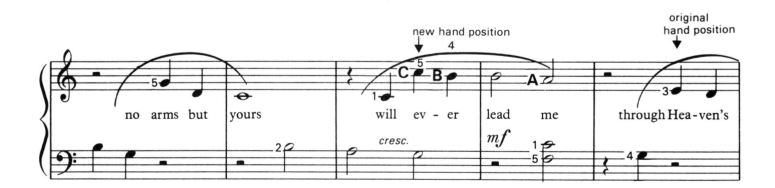

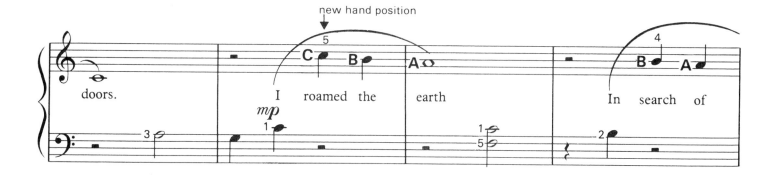

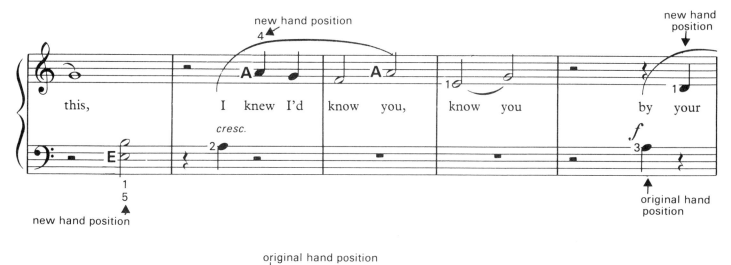

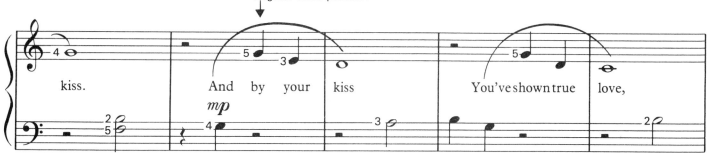

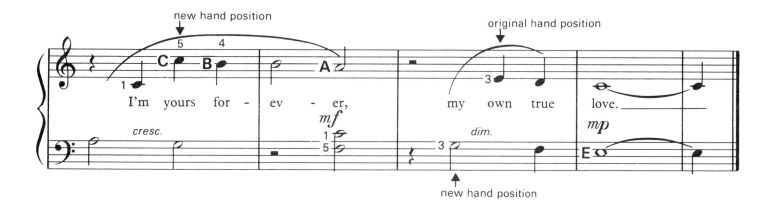

WOODEN HEART

Words & Music by Fred Wise, Ben Weisman,
Kay Twomey and Berthold Kaempfert.

Change hand positions smoothly

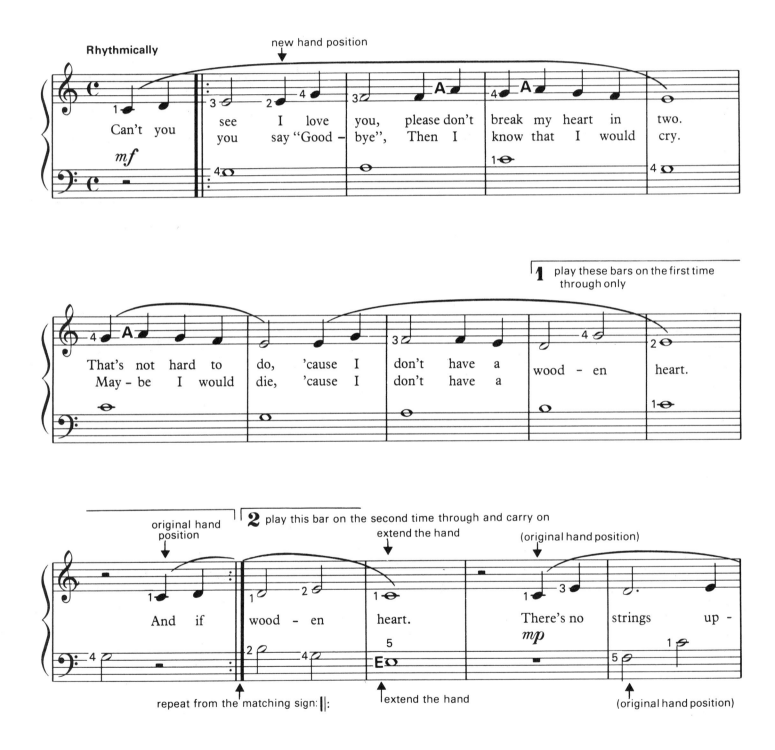

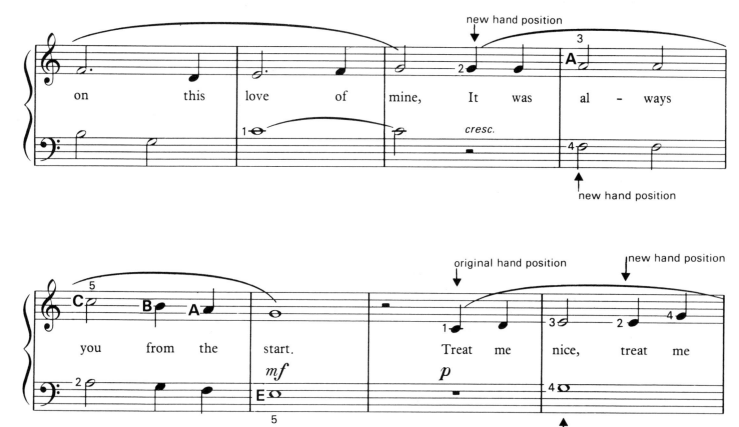

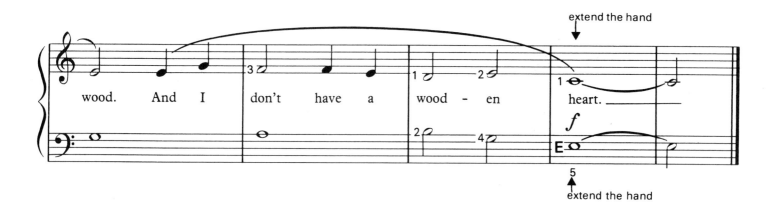

From now on I leave it to you to watch out for hand extensions and changes of hand position. Follow the printed fingering carefully and you can't go wrong.

DANNY BOY
Traditional

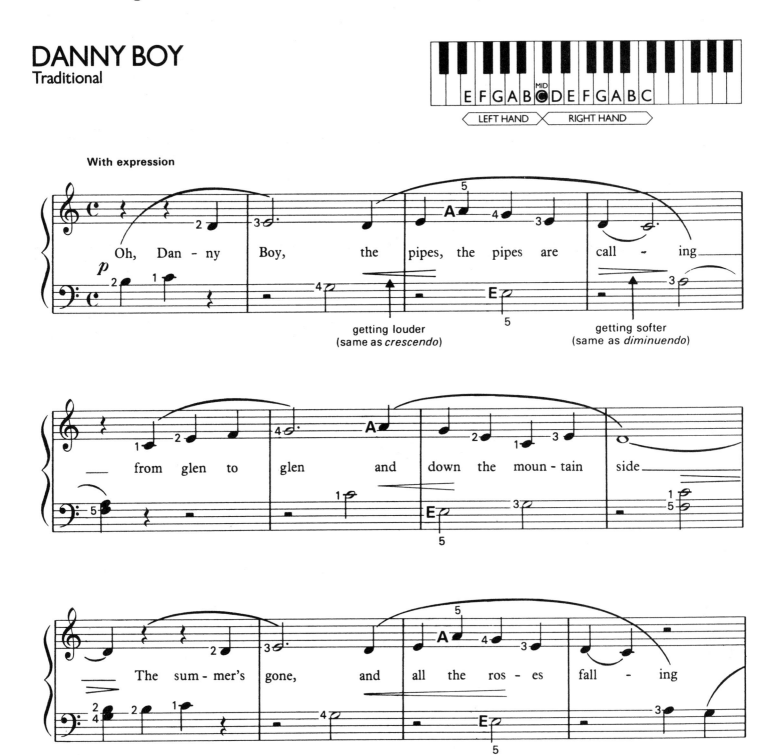

It's you, it's you must go and I must bide.

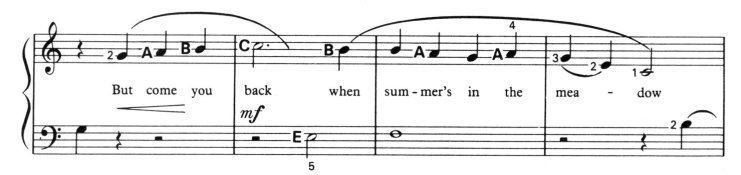

But come you back when sum-mer's in the mea-dow

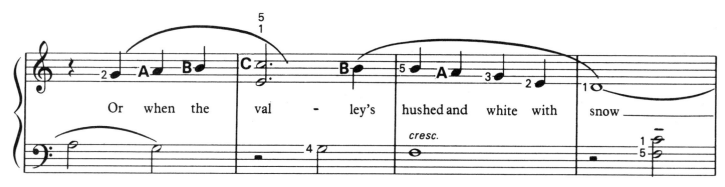

Or when the val-ley's hushed and white with snow ___

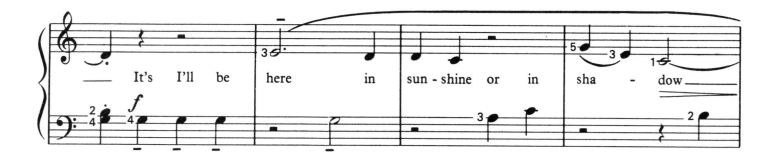

___ It's I'll be here in sun-shine or in sha-dow ___

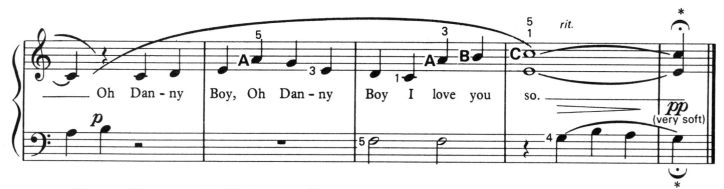

___ Oh Dan-ny Boy, Oh Dan-ny Boy I love you so.

*Pause (Fermata). Hold the note(s)
longer than written (at the discretion of
the player).

SHARPS AND NATURALS

2

This sign is called a sharp: ♯ Whenever you see a sharp written in front of a note, it means that you must play the nearest available key to the right of that note. This key may be **black or white.**

You continue to play the sharp throughout the bar, but it is automatically cancelled at the next bar.

Another way of cancelling a sharp is by writing a 'natural' sign against the note. The natural sign is written like this: ♮ For an example of the use of a natural sign, see bar 15 of *Puff The Magic Dragon*.

The most commonly used sharp is:

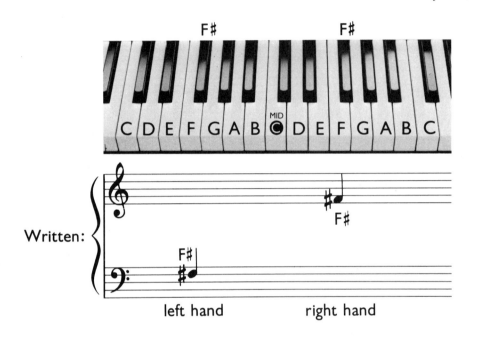

Written:

left hand   right hand

EXAMPLES OF OTHER SHARPS

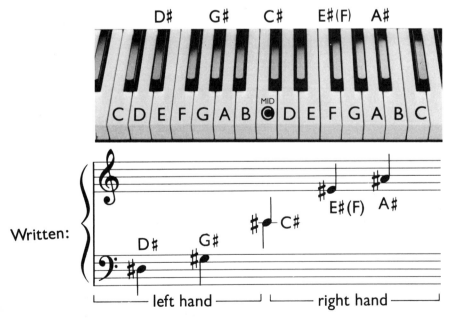

Written:

left hand ———— right hand ————

Notice that E♯ and F are exactly the same note. Sometimes it is more convenient to call F 'E♯'

PUFF (THE MAGIC DRAGON)

Words & Music by: Peter Yarrow and Leonard Lipton

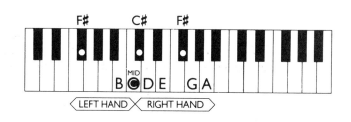

Watch out for 'sharp' notes in this piece. Remember to return to 'natural' notes.

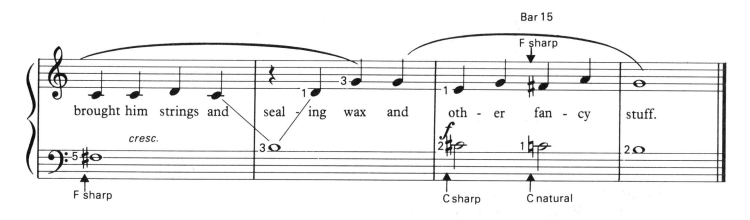

METRONOME MARKS

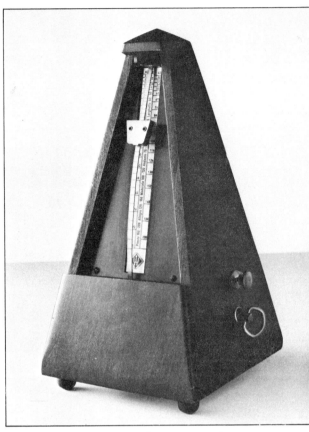

clockwork metronome

electronic metronome

A metronome is an instrument which indicates the speed of a piece of music.

The metronome mark: ♩ = 176 at the beginning of the next piece means that there are to be 176 quarter notes a minute (rather fast).
Set the pendulum to 176 and the instrument will "tick" at the correct speed. Don't leave the metronome running during your piece. Once you have the "feel" of the correct speed, turn it off.

CHORD SYMBOLS

From now on chord symbols will be included in all pieces. These symbols are intended for other instrumentalists, such as guitarists, who may wish to accompany you.

LAUGHING SAMBA

Words: Benny Meroff & Anne Spear.
Music: Vincent Rizzo & George Johnson.

Brightly ♩ = 176

C   Dm

Fun - ny   lit - tle   "Song - a",   some-thing like   a   Con - ga,
Ev' - ry   one   can   do   it,   there is   noth - ing   to   it,

mf

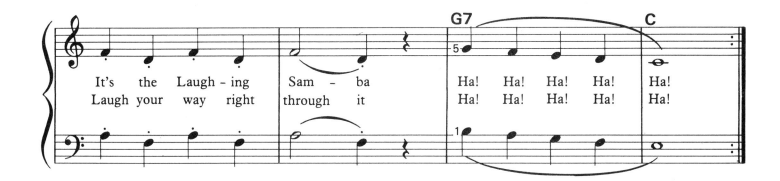

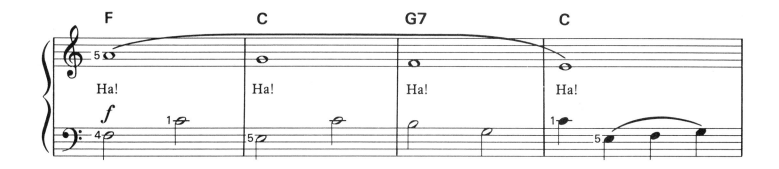

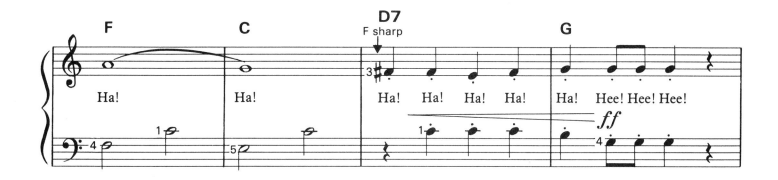

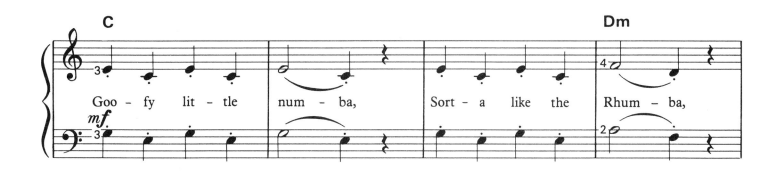

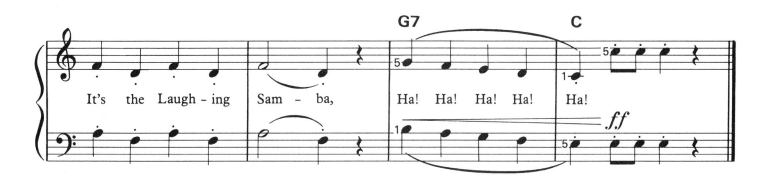

FLATS

4

A flat: ♭ in front of a note means play the nearest available key (black or white) to the left of that note.

The flat continues through the bar but is cancelled automatically at the next bar.

A 'natural': ♮ may also be used to cancel a flat.

The most commonly used flat is:

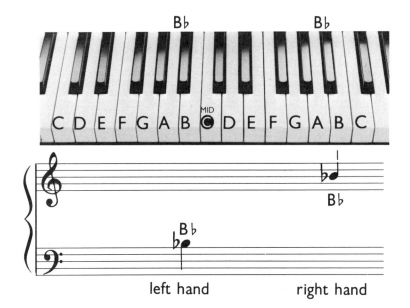

EXAMPLES OF OTHER FLATS

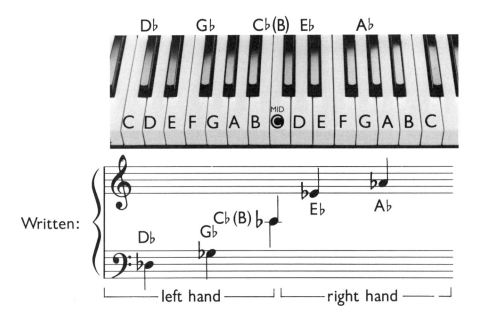

Notice that C♭ and B are exactly the same note. Sometimes it is more convenient to call B 'C♭'

LET HIM GO, LET HIM TARRY

Traditional

Watch out for 'flat' notes in this and the following piece. Remember to return to 'natural' notes.

Here the melody is taken over briefly by the left hand.

THE WINNER TAKES IT ALL

Words & Music: Benny Andersson & Bjorn Ulvaeus

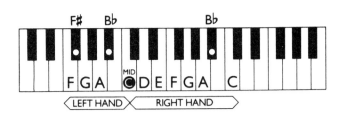

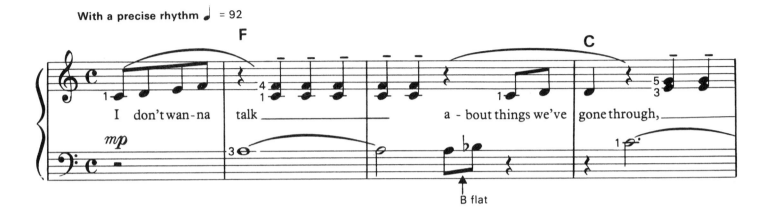

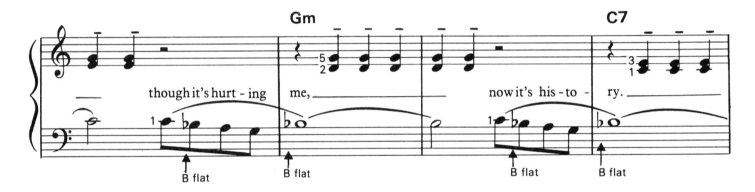

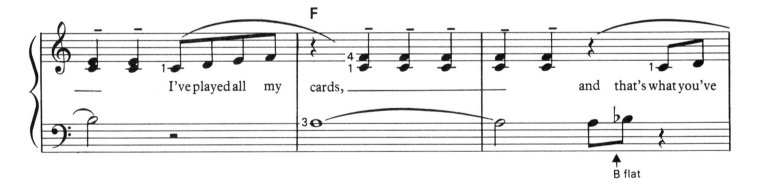

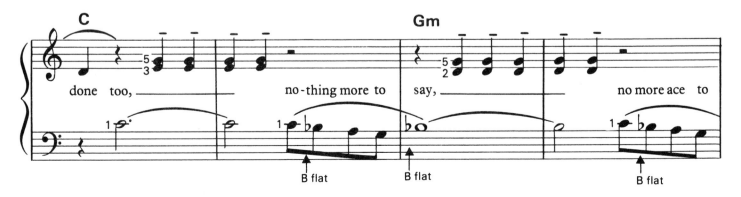

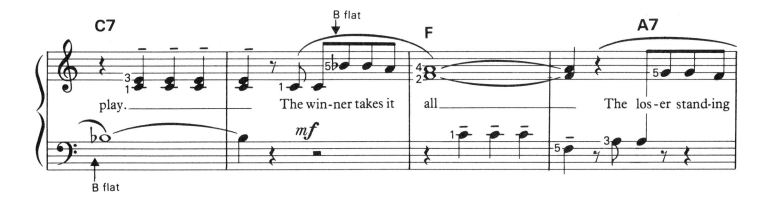

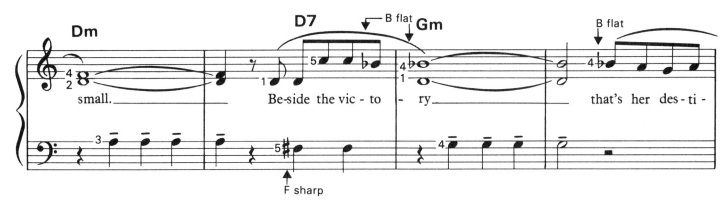

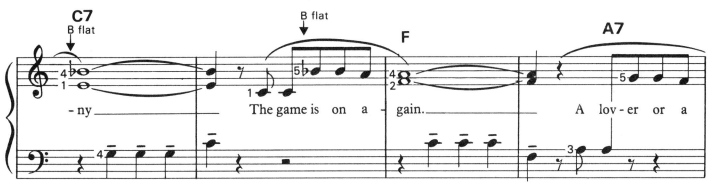

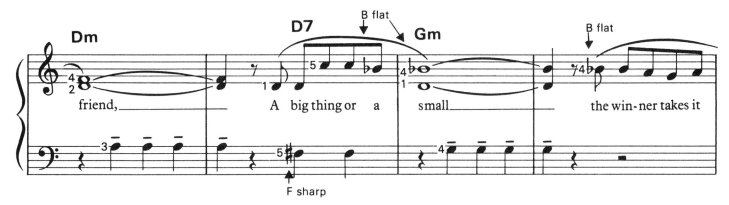

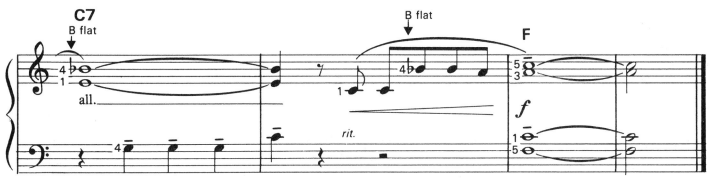

NEW NOTES

5

You are now going to learn a famous song by The Beatles. But before you tackle it, here are two new notes:

D for right hand
D for left hand

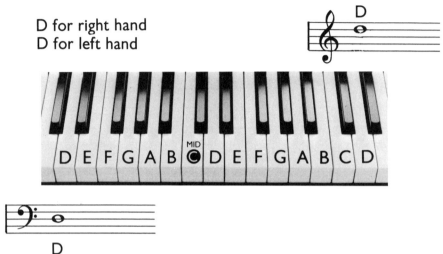

Both these notes – which are shown above – occur in your new piece, so make sure you know them.

A HARD DAY'S NIGHT

Words & Music: John Lennon and Paul McCartney

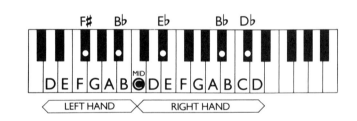

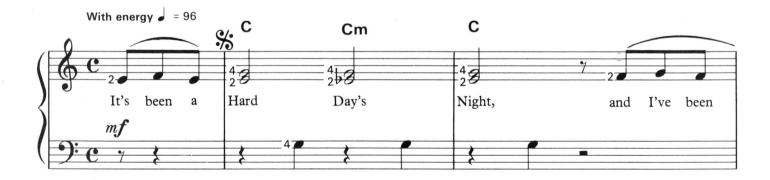

With energy ♩ = 96

It's been a Hard Day's Night, and I've been

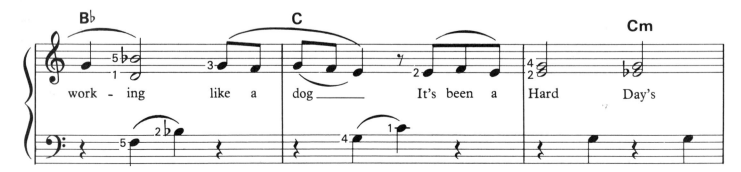

work - ing like a dog ____ It's been a Hard Day's

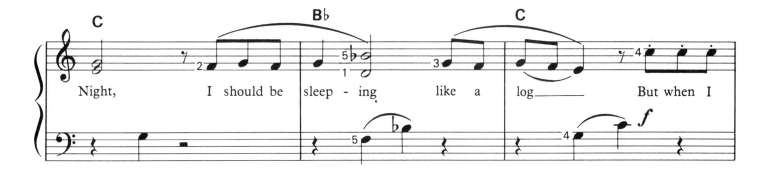

Night,   I should be sleep-ing like a log_____ But when I

get home to you, I find the things that you do will make me feel____ all____

right. When I'm home ev'-ry-thing seems to be

right_____ when I'm home

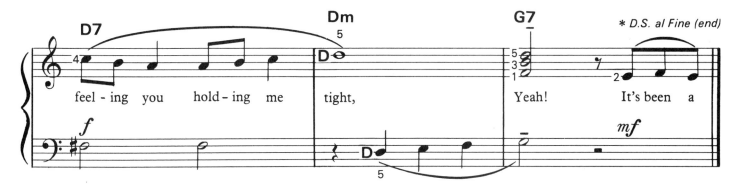

feel-ing you hold-ing me tight, Yeah! It's been a

*Dal Segno al Fine. 'From the sign to the end'. Go back to the sign 𝄋 and continue playing until 'Fine' (the end of the piece).

SCALE OF C, KEY OF C, PASSING NOTES

6

A 'Scale' is a succession of adjoining notes ascending or descending.

The 'Scale of C (Major)' requires no black notes:

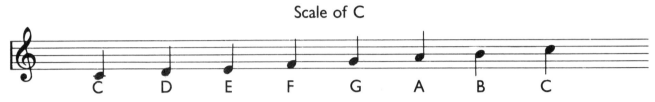

Scale of C

C D E F G A B C

When the notes used in a piece of music are all taken from the Scale of C, the piece is said to be in the 'Key of C'.

PASSING NOTES

However, a piece of music in C could use notes which are not in the Scale of C. If these notes are brief they are called 'passing notes'. Passing notes are of a temporary nature only and do not affect the overall key. The following arrangement of *Edelweiss* is an example of a piece in the key of C which uses black 'passing notes' in the harmony.

EDELWEISS
(FROM 'THE SOUND OF MUSIC')

Words by Oscar Hammerstein II.
Music by Richard Rodgers.

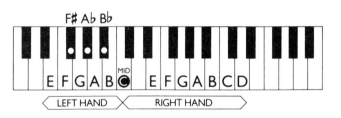

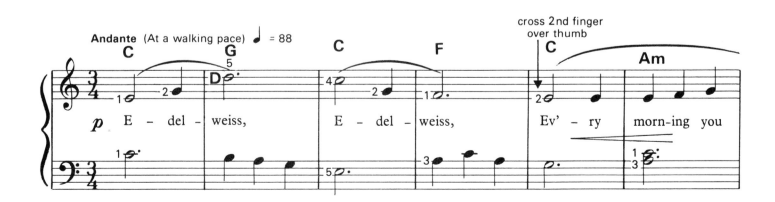

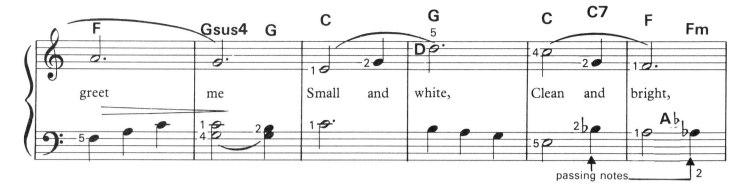

greet me Small and white, Clean and bright,

passing notes

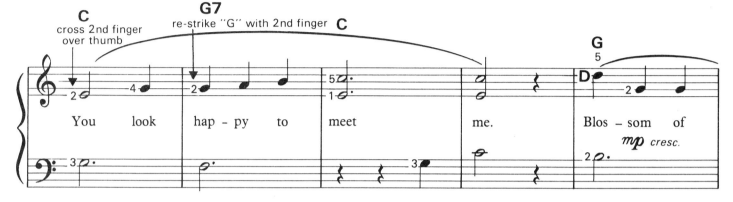

You look hap-py to meet me. Blos-som of

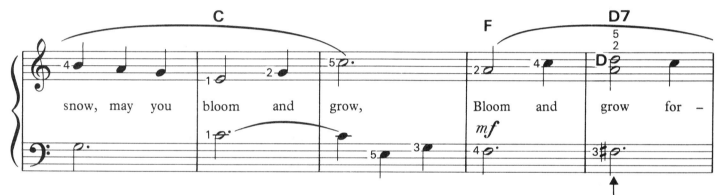

snow, may you bloom and grow, Bloom and grow for-

— ev — er. E — del — weiss, E — del —

passing note

cross 2nd finger over thumb   passing note

— weiss, Bless my home-land for — ev — er.

passing note

COMMON TIME AND
CUT COMMON TIME (ALLA BREVE)

7

The sign **C** stands for **4/4** time, that is, there are four quarter notes to the bar. **4/4** is also known as 'Common Time'.

The sign **₵** stands for **2/2** time, that is, there are two half notes to the bar,

2/2 time is also known as 'Cut Time', or Alla Breve.

Pieces written in Cut Time have a distinct feel of two in a bar, and they tend to be faster than those written in Common Time.

DO-RE-MI
(FROM 'THE SOUND OF MUSIC')

Words by Oscar Hammerstein II.
Music by Richard Rodgers.

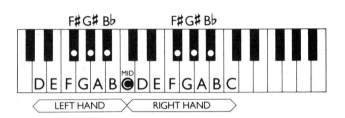

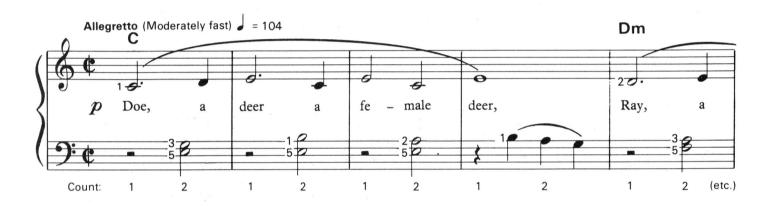

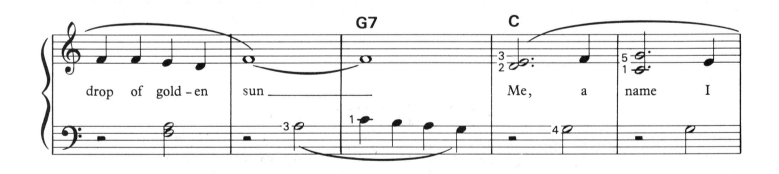

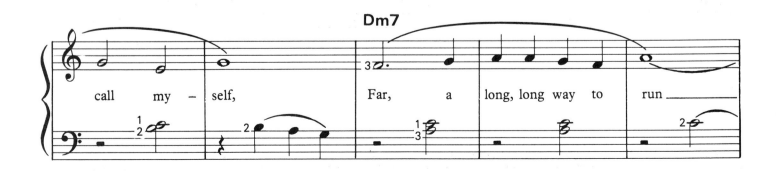

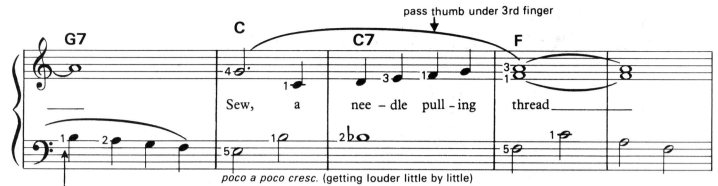

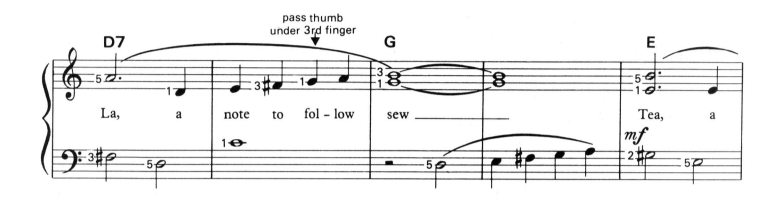

poco a poco cresc. (getting louder little by little)

SCALE OF F, KEY OF F, KEY SIGNATURE

8 Read lesson 6 again to refresh your memory about Scales, Keys, and Passing Notes.

The Key of F (Major) comes from the Scale of F (Major), which has one black note: B flat.

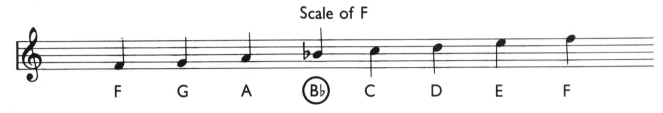

Pieces which are written in the Key of F (major) use the notes from the scale of the same name, although the piece may also include some passing notes.

When a piece is written in the key of F (major), it is necessary to indicate the B flats at the beginning of the piece, like this:

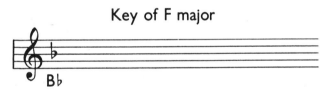

This is called the 'Key Signature'. It tells you that whenever you see the note B, you play it as B flat.

Under The Bridges Of Paris, which you are going to play now, is in the Key of F major, as you can see from the key signature.

Remember: you play all B's as B flats wherever they fall on the keyboard.

A REMINDER ABOUT NATURALS

A 'natural' sign: ♮ cancels a sharp or flat. The natural continues through the bar, but at the next bar everything reverts to normal.

UNDER THE BRIDGES OF PARIS
(SOUS LES PONTS DE PARIS)
Music: Vincent Scotto. English lyric: Dorcas Cochran.
French lyric: J. Rodor.

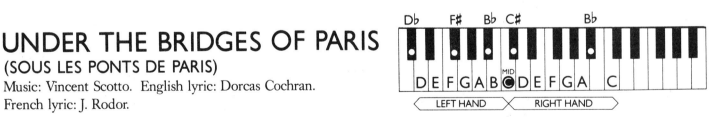

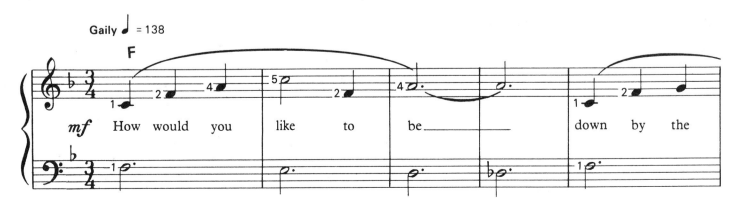

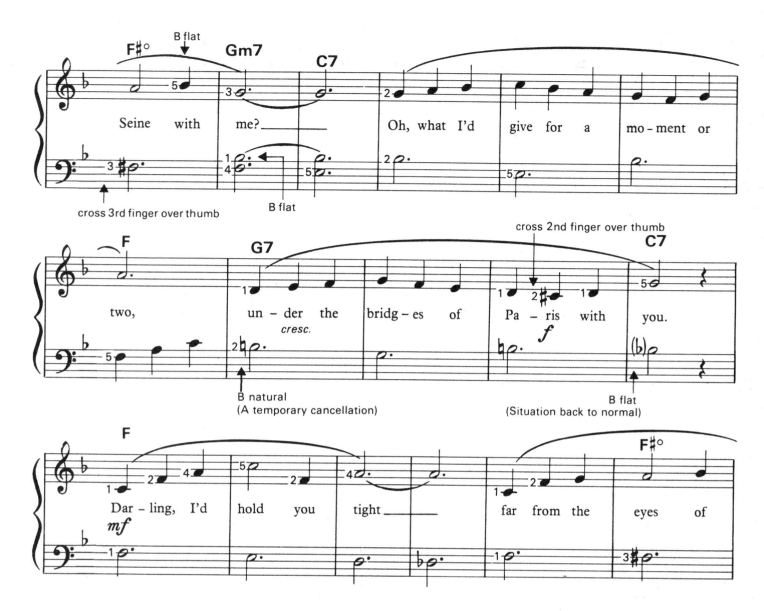

cross 3rd finger over thumb

B flat

cross 2nd finger over thumb

B natural
(A temporary cancellation)

B flat
(Situation back to normal)

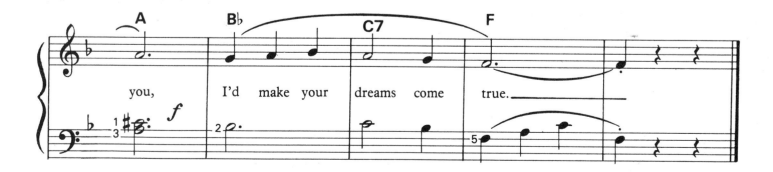

Seine with me? Oh, what I'd give for a mo-ment or two, un-der the bridg-es of Pa-ris with you. Dar-ling, I'd hold you tight far from the eyes of night Un-der the bridg-es of Pa-ris with you, I'd make your dreams come true.

LIEBESTRÄUME

By: Franz Liszt

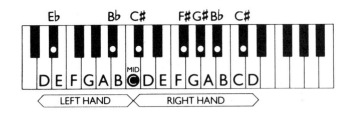

Remember: **This solo is in F major.**
Play all B's as B flats, unless
instructed otherwise.

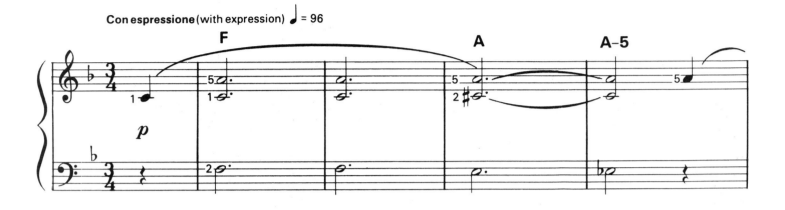

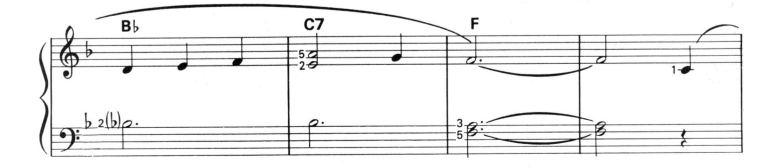

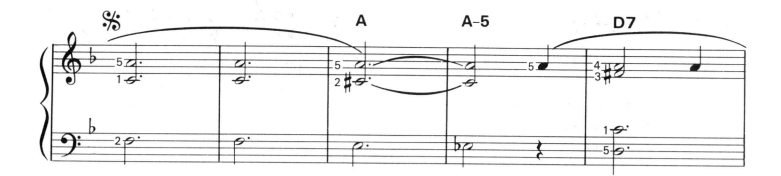

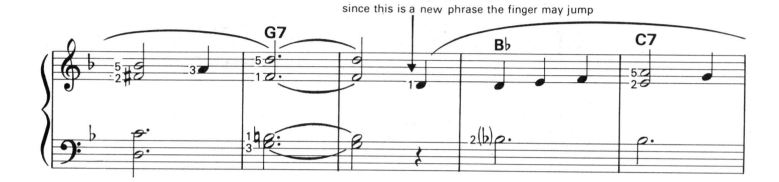

since this is a new phrase the finger may jump

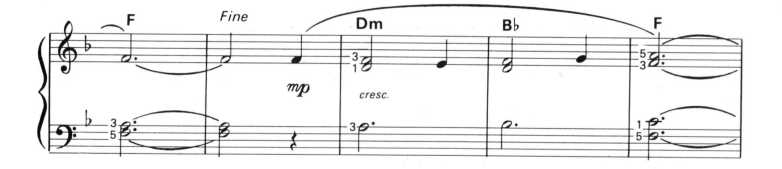

Fine

change to 3rd finger on A

D.S. al Fine

In Time i.e. pick up the original speed

BRIGHT EYES

Words & Music: Mike Batt

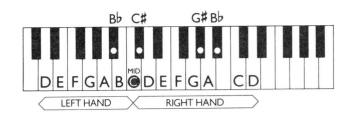

Remember: All B's are to be played as
B flats, unless instructed otherwise.

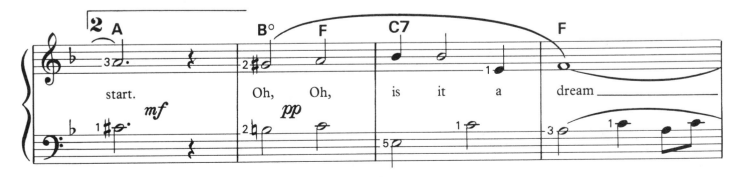

*Repeat Marking. Since there is no
matching Repeat Sign to go back to,
repeat from the beginning of the piece.

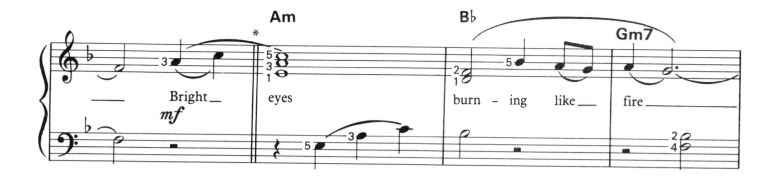

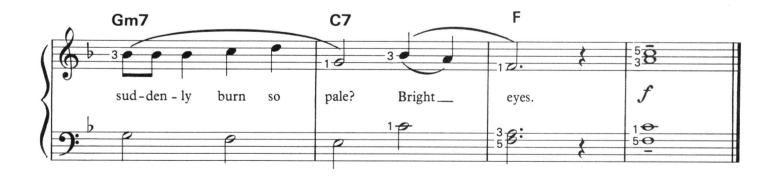

*Section Lines. End of one Section of the piece and the beginning of another.

NEW NOTES

9 Before tackling the next two pieces, here are some new notes for you to learn. Make sure that you can recognize them as soon as you see them, by practising them a few times:

E, F for right hand
C for left hand

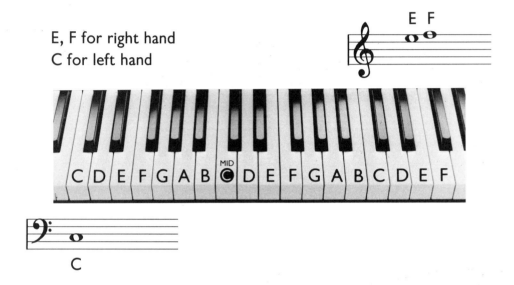

C

PLAISIR D'AMOUR
Words & Music: Giovanni Paolo Martini

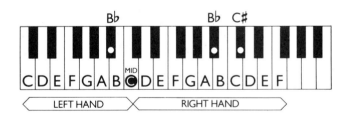

Con espressione ♩ = 100

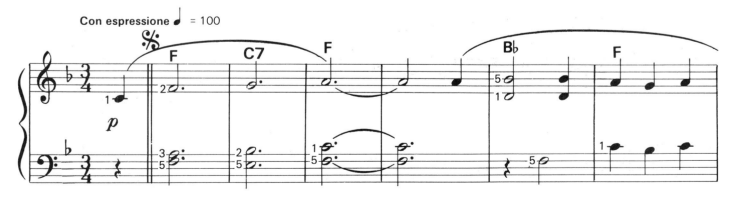

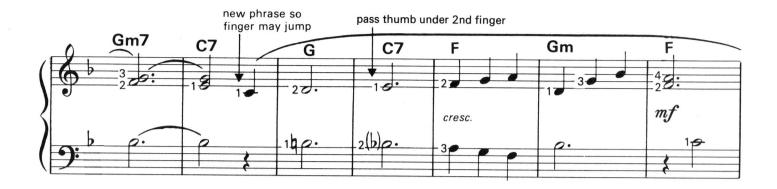

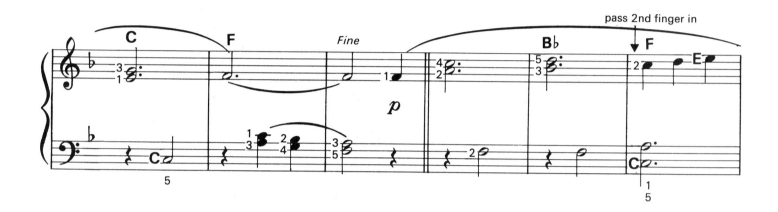

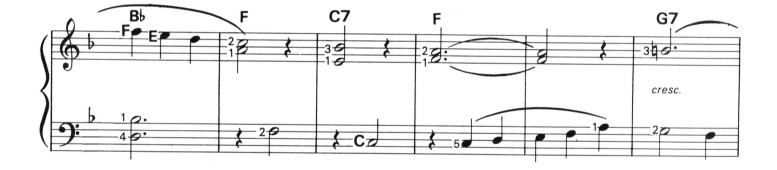

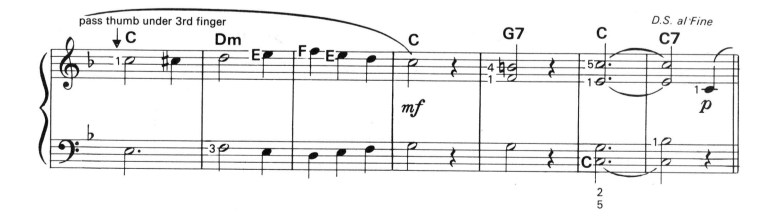

TAKE ME HOME, COUNTRY ROADS

Words & Music: Bill Danoff,
Taffy Nivert and John Denver

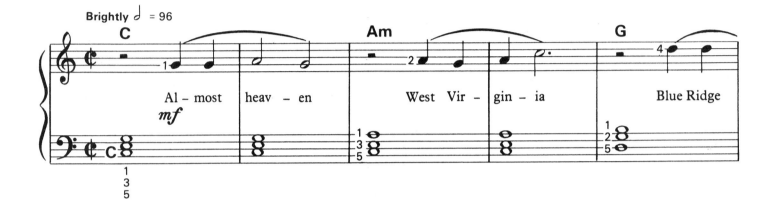

Al - most heav - en   West Vir - gin - ia   Blue Ridge

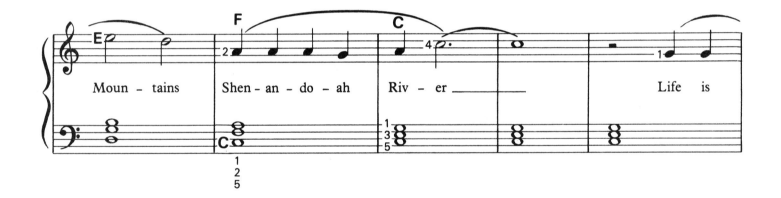

Moun - tains   Shen - an - do - ah   Riv - er ____   Life is

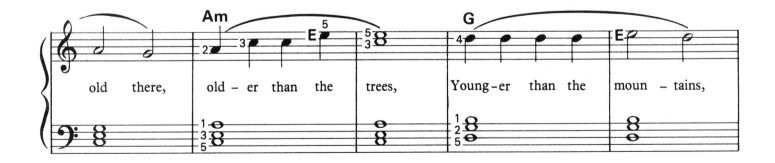

old there,   old - er than the trees,   Young - er than the   moun - tains,

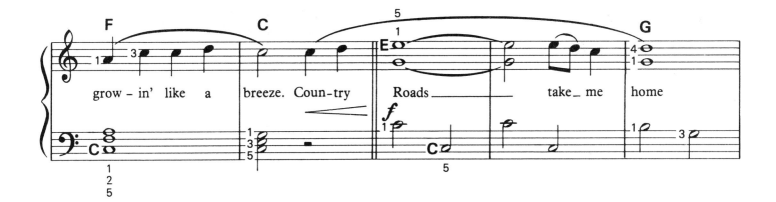

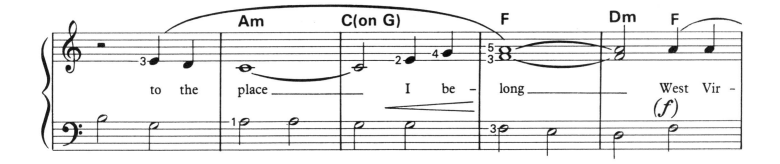

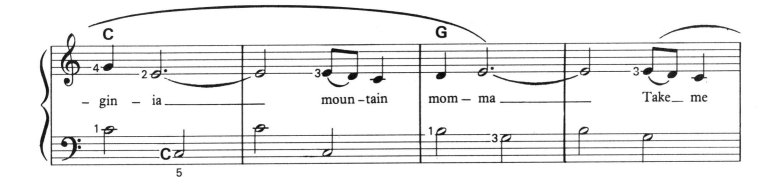

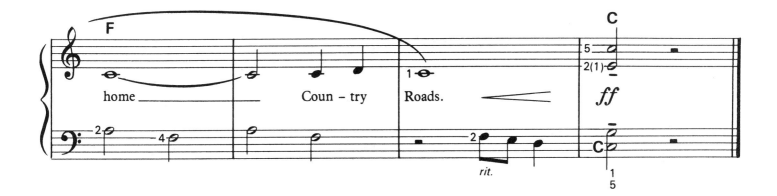

DOTTED QUARTER NOTE

10

A dot after a note increases its value by one half. When you apply this principle to a quarter note you get:

♩ quarter note = 1 beat

♩. dotted quarter note = 1½ beats

A dotted quarter note (1½ beats) is almost always accompanied by a single eighth (½ beat), making two full quarter note beats in all:

♩. ♪ 1½ beats + ½ beat   Total: 2 beats
or:
♪ ♩. ½ beat + 1½ beats   Total: 2 beats

The first of these dotted quarter note/eighth note combinations: ♩. ♪ appears frequently in the piece that follows.
It is counted like this:

SILENT NIGHT

count: 1   2 and 3   1   2   3

Pick a suitable speed for your basic quarter note beat **and be sure to maintain the same speed throughout the piece.**

BAR 1
● Play 'G' on beat 1 and let the sound continue as you count beat 2.
● Play 'A' on the 'and' between beats 2 and 3.
● Play 'G' on beat 3.

BAR 2
● Play 'E' on beat 1 and let the sound continue through beats 2 and 3.

Continue similarly through the piece.

LEFT HAND MELODY

Notice that during Bars 9-16 of *Silent Night* the Left Hand plays the melody. Increase the volume of the Left Hand at this point so that the melody can be heard clearly.

SILENT NIGHT

Words & Music: Joseph Mohr and Franz Gruber

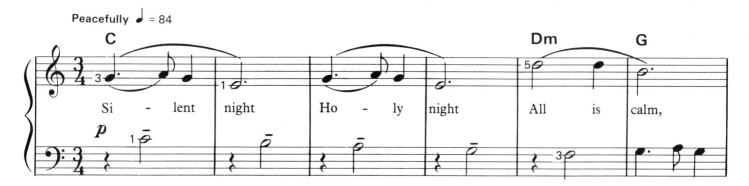

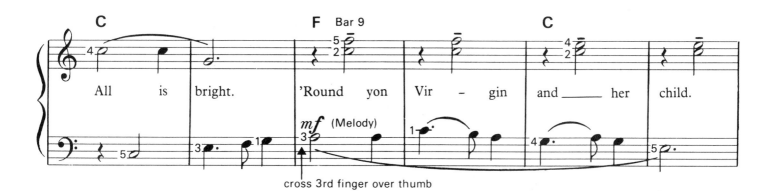

cross 3rd finger over thumb

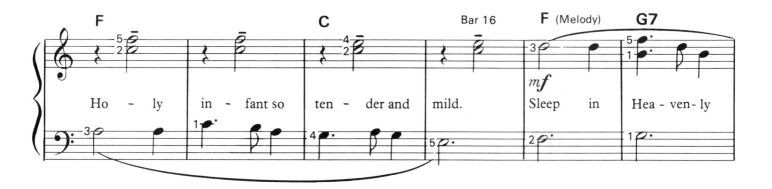

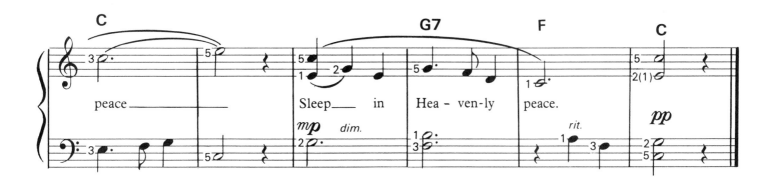

DOTTED QUARTER NOTE–2

The next song features the second of our dotted quarter note/eighth note combinations.
This time the eighth note is played first:

♪♩. ½ beat + 1½ beats Total: 2 beats

Count this figure like this:

GUANTANAMERA

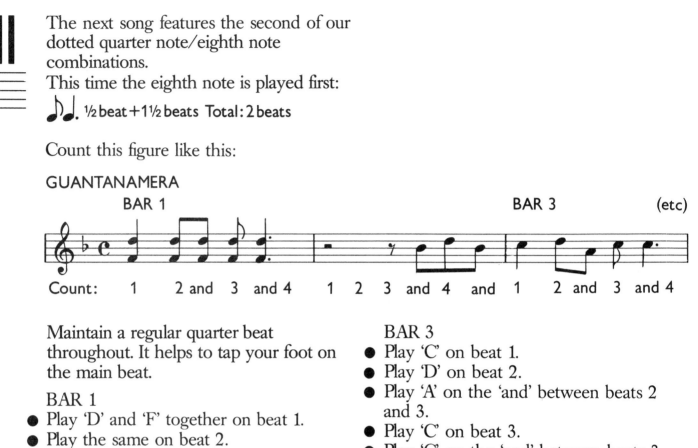

Count: 1 2 and 3 and 4   1 2 3 and 4 and   1 2 and 3 and 4

Maintain a regular quarter beat throughout. It helps to tap your foot on the main beat.

BAR 1
● Play 'D' and 'F' together on beat 1.
● Play the same on beat 2.
● Play the same on the 'and' between beats 2 and 3.
● Play the same on beat 3.
● Play the same on the 'and' between beats 3 and 4.
● Let the sound continue through beat 4.

BAR 3
● Play 'C' on beat 1.
● Play 'D' on beat 2.
● Play 'A' on the 'and' between beats 2 and 3.
● Play 'C' on beat 3.
● Play 'C' on the 'and' between beats 3 and 4.
● Let the sound continue through beat 4.

Continue like this through the piece.

GUANTANAMERA

Words by: Jose Marti.
Music adaptation by: Hector Angulo and Pete Seeger.

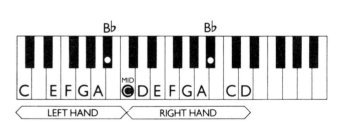

With a gentle rhythm ♩ = 92

Guan - ta - na - me - ra   gua - ji - ra   Guan - ta - na - me - ra

Teachers: * The flat has been put here for the moment because the pupil has not been taught the lower 'B' note. The normal F major key signature appears in Book 3, page 12.

cross 3rd finger over thumb

cross 2nd finger over thumb

Guan - ta - na - me - ra   gua-ji - ra   Guan-ta-na-me - ra!   Yo soy un

cross 2nd finger over thumb

hom - bre sin-ce - ro   De don-de   cre - ce la pal-ma   Yo soy un

hom - bre sin-ce - ro   De don-de   cre - ce la   pal - ma.   Yan-tes de

*D.C. al Fine

mo - rir - me quie - ro,   E - char mis   ver - sos del al - ma

*Da Capo al Fine 'From the beginning to the end'. Go back to the beginning of the piece and continue playing until 'Fine' (the end of the piece).

The next piece makes use of both the
♩. ♪ and ♪ ♩. dotted quarter note/eighth
note combinations.

BY THE TIME I GET TO PHOENIX

Words & Music: Jim Webb

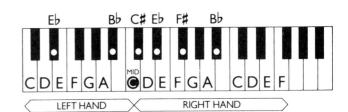

By the time I get to Phoe-nix___ she'll be ri-sin'

She'll

Count: 1 and 2 3 4 and 1 and 2 3 4 and

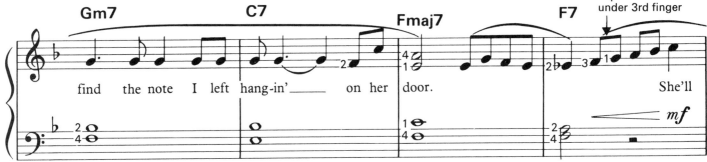

find the note I left hang-in'___ on her door.

She'll

laugh when she reads the part___ that says I'm leav-in'___ 'cause I've

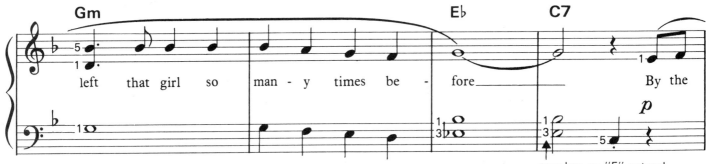

left that girl so man-y times be-fore___

By the

new bar, so "E" natural

42

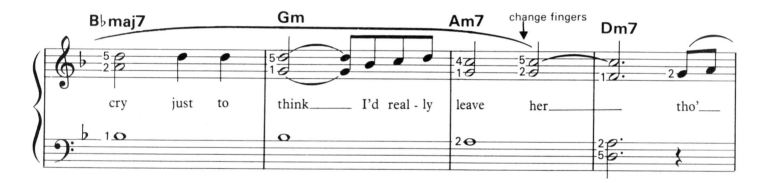

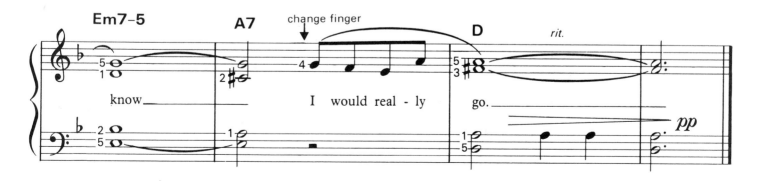

WRIST STACCATO

Hand in position to strike

Down stroke

Up stroke

Learning the following piece will give you practice in wrist staccato. After each note let your hand spring up from your wrist **without moving your arm.**

Keep your wrist flexible and you will always feel comfortable when using this technique.

WILLIAM TELL OVERTURE
(THEME FROM)

By: Gioacchino Rossini

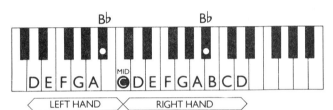

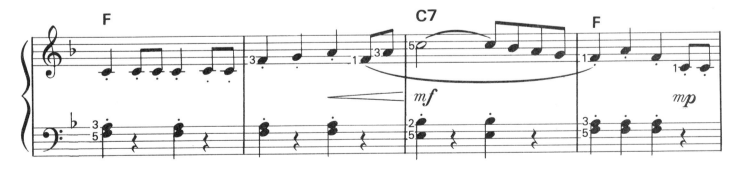

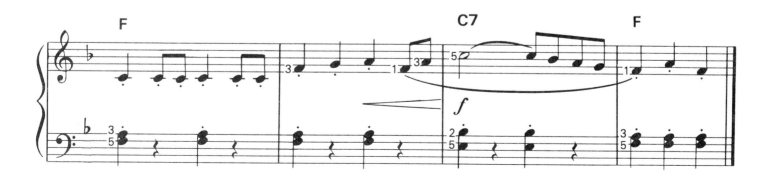

TWO TUNES WITH ONE HAND

13

Often in a piece of piano music there is a second tune accompanying the main tune. There may even be more than one secondary tune. These secondary tunes can be complete 'counter' melodies, or just short, melodic fragments put in to enhance the main melody. This is similar to choral music, where the singers are singing different tunes (or 'parts'), the whole blending together to create the 'harmony'.

On the piano, these secondary 'parts' tend to occur below, that is lower than, the main melody. Two parts are often played by one hand.

Look at bars 6 and 7 and bars 22, 23 and 24 of the following song. You will see examples of two different tunes, or parts, played by the right hand. Hold all lower notes for their full value and finger 'legato' in order to bring out the lower parts.

WHAT KIND OF FOOL AM I?
FROM THE MUSICAL PRODUCTION 'STOP THE WORLD I WANT TO GET OFF'.
Words & Music: Leslie Bricusse and Anthony Newley.

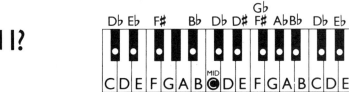

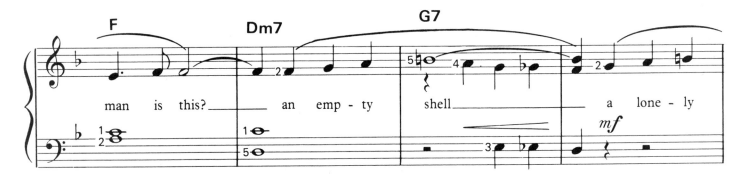

46

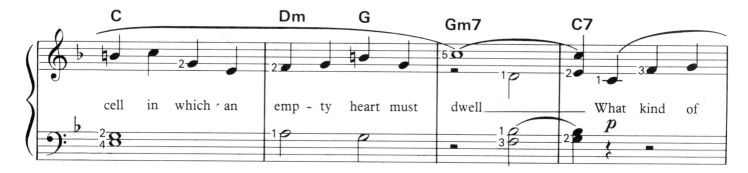

cell in which an emp - ty heart must dwell_____ What kind of

slide 2nd finger from black note to white

lips are these_____ that lied with ev - 'ry kiss?_____ That whis - pered

cresc.

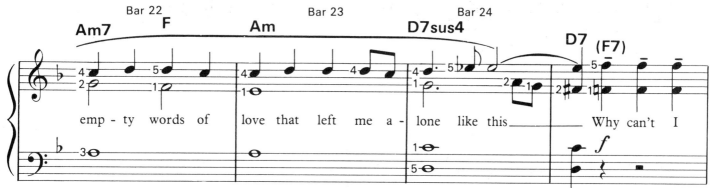

Bar 22   Bar 23   Bar 24

emp - ty words of love that left me a - lone like this_____ Why can't I

fall in love like an - y oth - er man? And may - be

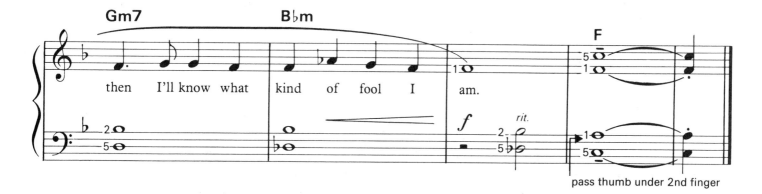

then I'll know what kind of fool I am.

rit.

pass thumb under 2nd finger

LAST WORD

Congratulations on reaching the end of Book 2 of The Complete Piano Player!

In Book Three you will be:
- Learning new notes
- Playing in different keys
- Discovering new left hand styles and rhythms
- Developing your piano technique

Till then your last song in this book is:

LET IT BE

Words & Music: John Lennon & Paul McCartney

THE COMPLETE PIANO PLAYER
BOOK 3

'By the end of this book you will understand
the importance of expression in music,
and will be playing 22 popular songs,
including: *Imagine, Blue Moon, Norwegian Wood,*
and *Raindrops Keep Fallin' On My Head*.'

Kenneth Baker

Amsco Publications
New York/London/Sydney

Exclusive Distributors:
Music Sales Corporation
257 Park Avenue South, New York, NY 10010, USA

This book Copyright © 1984 and 1985 by
Amsco Publications
Order No. AM 39645
International Standard Book Number: 0.8256.2439.8

Designed by Howard Brown
Photography by Peter Wood
Arranged by Kenneth Baker

Printed in the United States of America by
Vicks Lithograph and Printing Corporation

CONTENTS

ABOUT THIS BOOK

Now that you have successfully completed the first two books of The Complete Piano Player, you are ready to learn some styles which will make you "sound like a professional".

As before, all lessons are based on songs made famous by outstanding groups and stars, as well as on delightful classical pieces. Altogether there are twenty new songs and pieces to add to your already considerable repertoire.

You will also get plenty of practice in note reading, and your sense of timing and rhythm will become even more developed. Easy to follow text and clear diagrams, as usual, ensure that your progress is made as smooth as possible.

If you are working on your own, keep up regular practice every day. This is the way to achieve your aim of becoming a complete piano player.

TO TEACHERS

Book Three of The Complete Piano Player course follows the proven principles laid down in the first two books. Sound technique is taught throughout. Lessons are made enjoyable by basing them on music which keeps students interested throughout the entire course. As a course for teaching today's students, you will find The Complete Piano Player ideal.

CHORD PYRAMIDS

This is a simple yet effective type of accompaniment which can be used with most ballads (slow expressive tunes, often played with a rather flexible tempo).

Play the notes of the chord one by one with your left hand, holding each note down until the chord pyramid is formed. Observe the ties carefully.

SMILE

Words: John Turner & Geoffrey Parsons. Music: Charles Chaplin

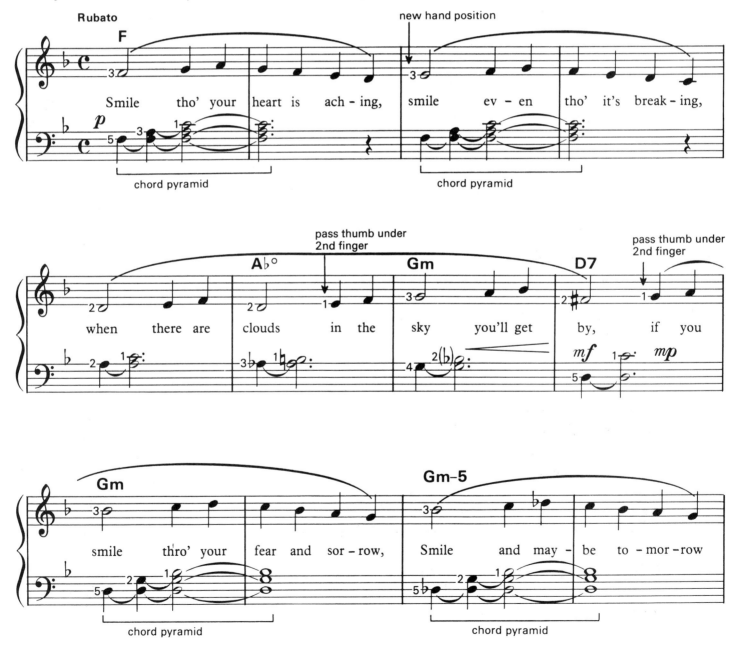

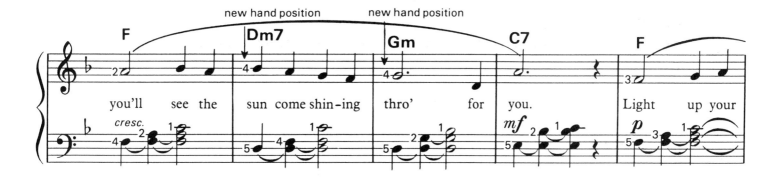

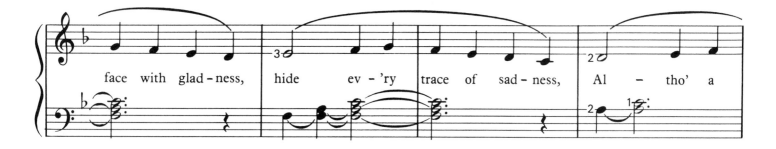

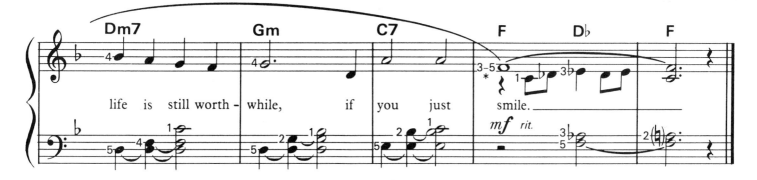

*Shift Technique. Sometimes necessary for good legato playing. Play F with 3rd finger then shift to 5th finger without releasing the note. The 3rd finger is now ready for use again in the next phrase.

The chord pyramid technique can often be used effectively in the right hand also, as seen in the following arrangement of *Fascination*.

FASCINATION

Music: F.D. Marchetti. English Lyric: Dick Manning

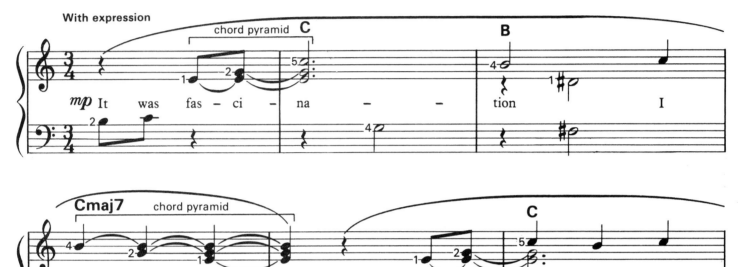

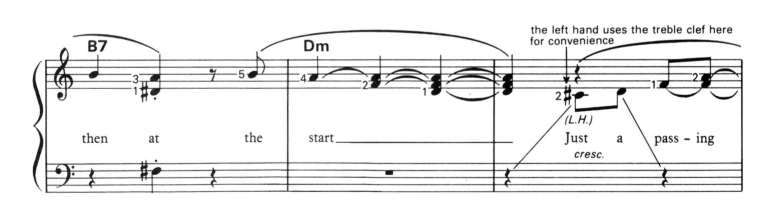

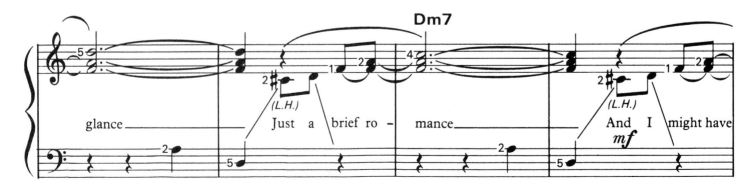

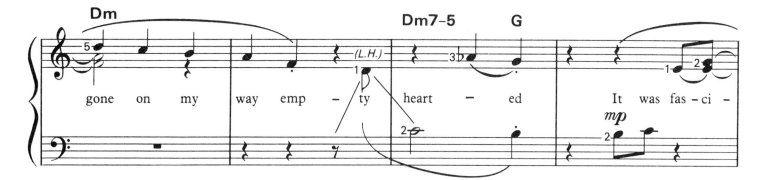

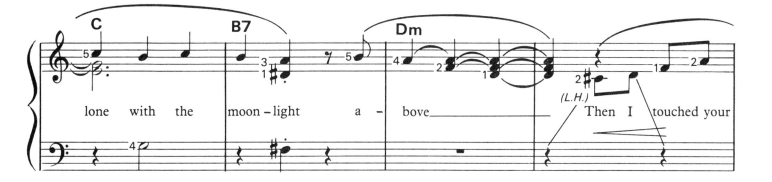

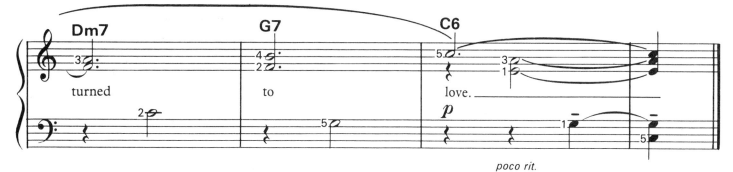

poco rit.

(a little ritenuto: slowing down slightly)

NEW NOTES

2

Before tackling the next song, here are
some new notes for you to learn:

G, A and low B for
right hand
F, G, A and B for
left hand

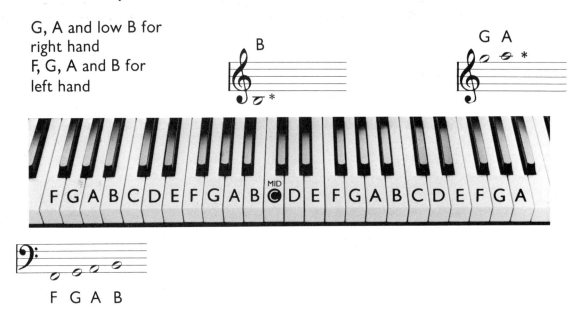

F G A B

ACCOMPANIMENT PATTERNS

Notice the repeated accompaniment
patterns in the left hand in *Spanish Eyes*.

SPANISH EYES

Words: Charles Singleton & Eddie Snyder. Music: Bert Kaempfert

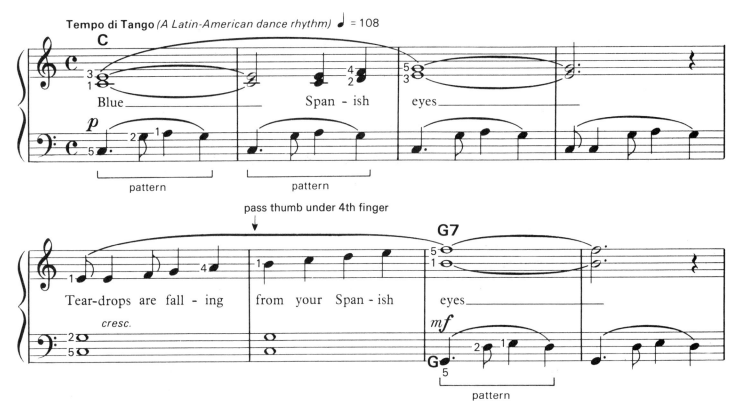

*Ledger line: A partial line used to
represent the full length line which

would lie in that position (see Book
One pages 15 and 16).

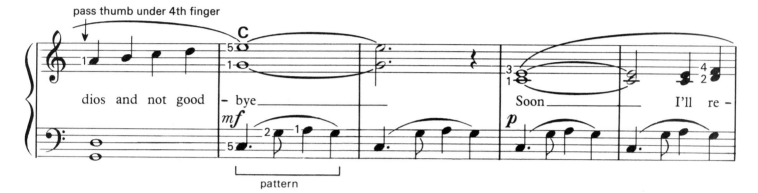

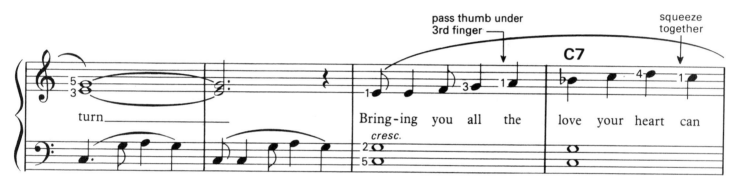

PHRASES AND PHRASING

3

A 'phrase' is a group of notes which belong together musically.
'Phrasing' refers to the way in which the notes are played.
Usually you play the notes of your phrases legato (connected):

SMILE (Book 3, p.6)

a legato phrase

Sometimes you play them staccato (disconnected):

Theme from WILLIAM TELL OVERTURE (Book 2, p.44)

a staccato phrase

In *I Whistle A Happy Tune*, you will be using a mixture of staccato and legato phrasing. You will also be accenting certain notes. Such different types of phrasing within a piece help to give it contrast, and contrast is one of the most important aspects of phrasing.

I WHISTLE A HAPPY TUNE
(FROM 'THE KING AND I')

Words: Oscar Hammerstein II. Music: Richard Rodgers

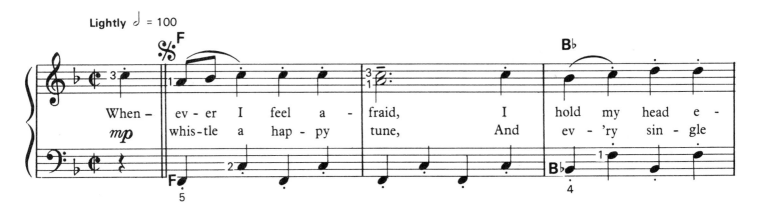

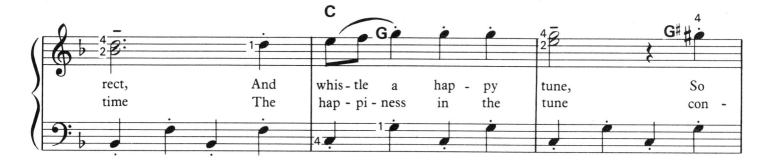

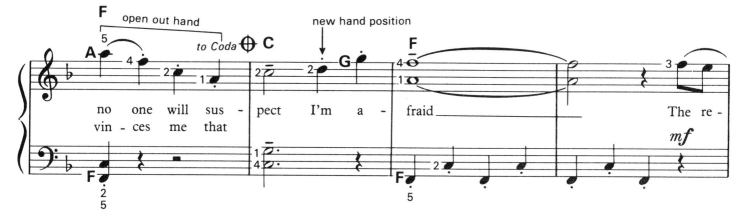

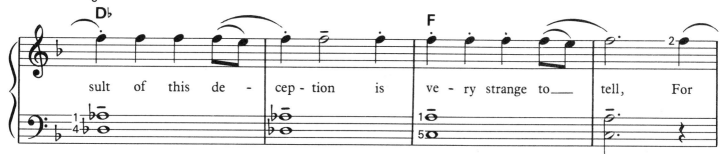

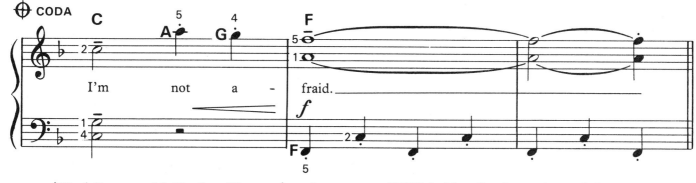

*Dal Segno Al Coda : 'From the sign to Coda'. Repeat from the sign (𝄋) until 'to Coda ⊕ '. From there jump to CODA (the final section of the piece) and play through to the end.

KEY OF G

The key of G (Major) is derived from the scale of G (Major), which requires one black note: F sharp:

Scale of G

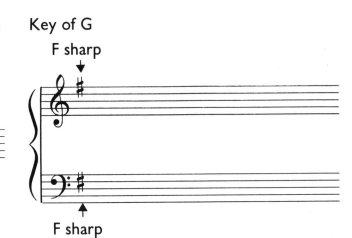

G A B C D E (F#) G

Pieces using this scale predominantly are said to be in the key of G.
The key signature for the key of G is:

Key of G

When you are in this key you must remember to play every F (wherever it might fall on the keyboard) as F sharp.

BLUE MOON
Words: Lorenz Hart. Music: Richard Rodgers

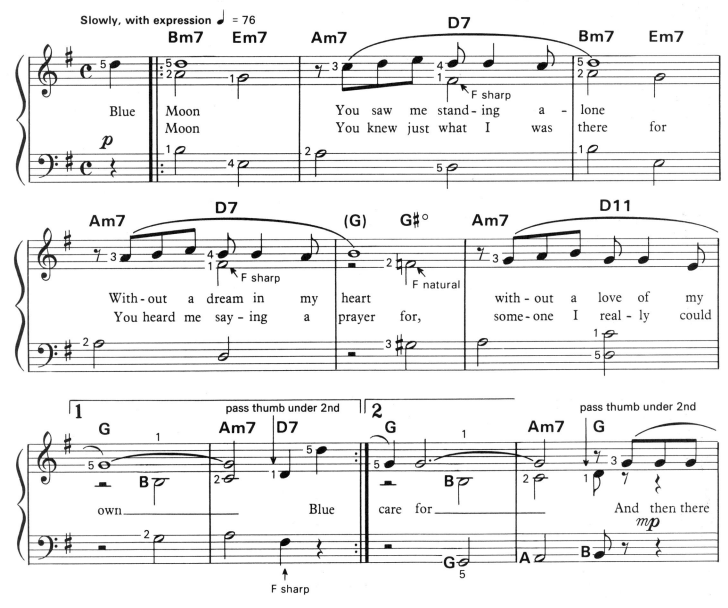

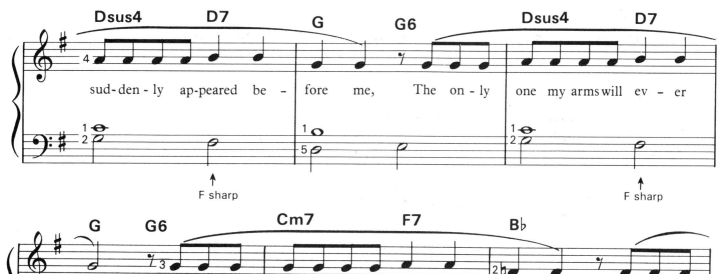

sud-den - ly ap-peared be - fore me, The on - ly one my arms will ev - er

F sharp F sharp

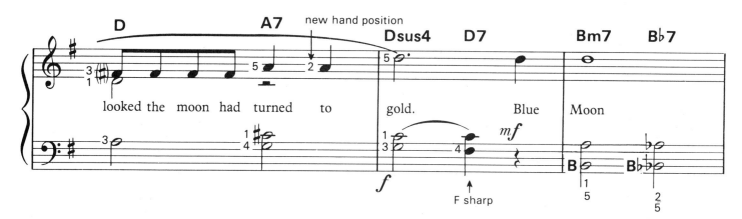

hold I heard some - bo - dy whis-per "please a - dore me," And when I

cresc.

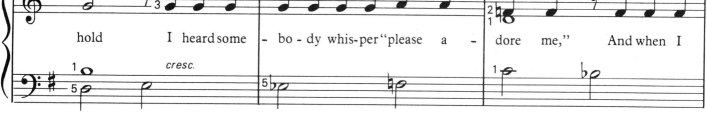

looked the moon had turned to gold. Blue Moon

new hand position

F sharp

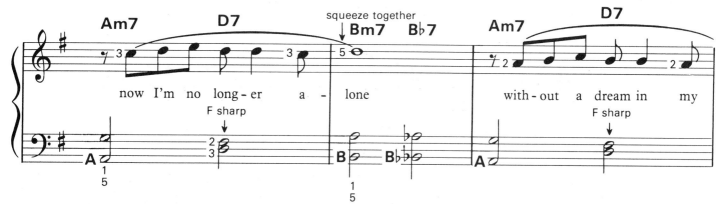

now I'm no long-er a - lone with - out a dream in my

squeeze together

F sharp F sharp

squeeze together new hand position

heart with - out a love of my own.

$\frac{6}{8}$ TIME

5

This means six eighth notes, or their equivalent, per bar.

In $\frac{6}{8}$ time the dotted quarter note ♩. is the basic beat, and there are two dotted quarter notes per bar:

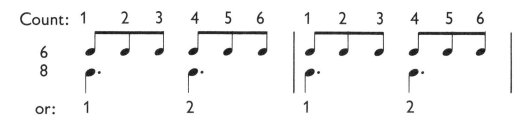

The player may count either 6 eighth notes or 2 dotted quarter notes per bar, whichever is more convenient.

In slow pieces e.g. *Greensleeves* (p.17) it will probably be more convenient to count 6 in a bar:

GREENSLEEVES

Start playing here

In faster pieces e.g. *Liberty Bell* (p.20) it will probably be better to count 2 in a bar:

LIBERTY BELL

GREENSLEEVES
Traditional

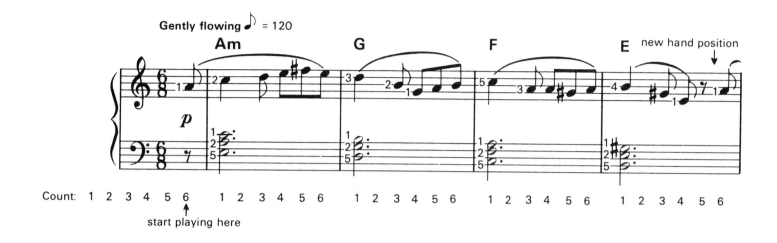

Count: 1 2 3 4 5 6 1 2 3 4 5 6 1 2 3 4 5 6 1 2 3 4 5 6 1 2 3 4 5 6

start playing here

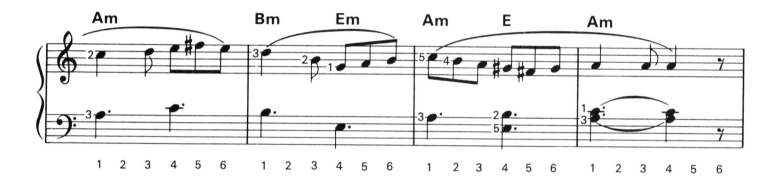

1 2 3 4 5 6   1 2 3 4 5 6   1 2 3 4 5 6   1 2 3 4 5 6

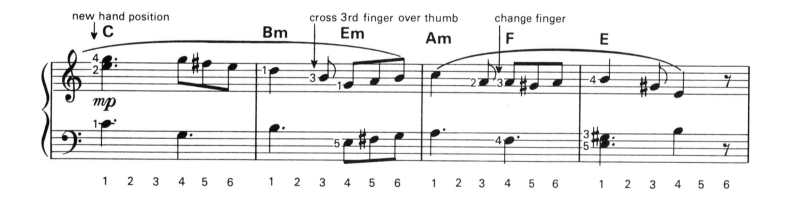

1 2 3 4 5 6   1 2 3 4 5 6   1 2 3 4 5 6   1 2 3 4 5 6

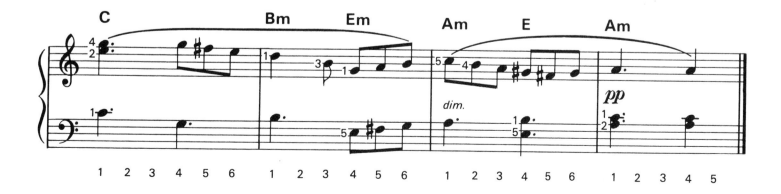

1 2 3 4 5 6   1 2 3 4 5 6   1 2 3 4 5 6   1 2 3 4 5

THE TWO-NOTE SLUR

6

You learned in Book One (p. 36) that a slur, sometimes called a phrase mark, is a curved line covering the notes, indicating that they are to be played legato:

play legato

When a slur covers two notes only:

stress the first note (play slightly louder); let the second note be weak (play softer and staccato).

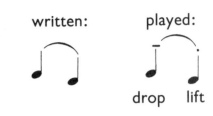

written: played:

drop   lift

Let your hand *drop* onto the first note and *lift* up from the second note. This will give you the correct sound of the two-note slur.

I have arrowed the two-note slurs in the following piece.

NORWEGIAN WOOD
(THIS BIRD HAS FLOWN)

Words & Music: John Lennon and Paul McCartney

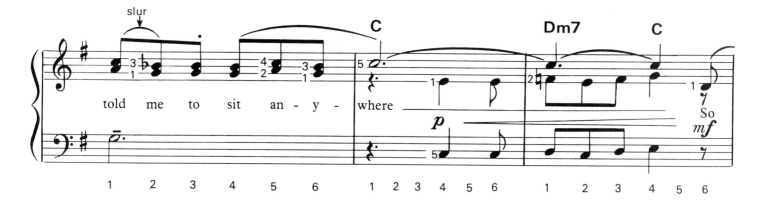

told me to sit an-y-where

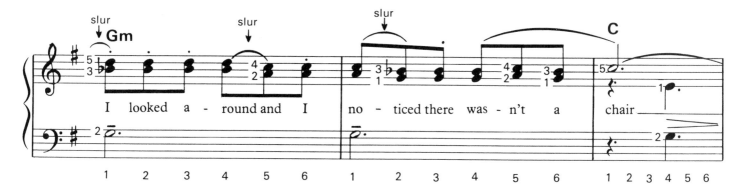

I looked a-round and I no-ticed there was-n't a chair

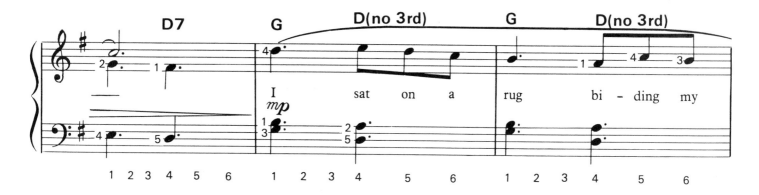

I sat on a rug bi-ding my

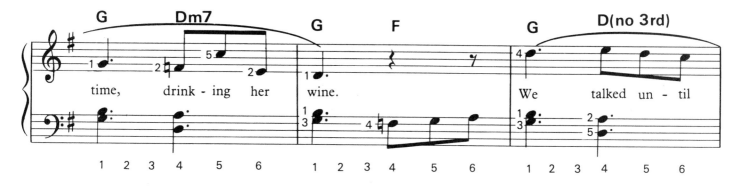

time, drink-ing her wine. We talked un-til

two and then she said: "It's time for bed".

(Pause)

NEW NOTE

7

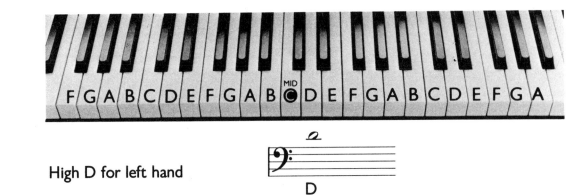

High D for left hand

Look for the new D note in the following three pieces.

LIBERTY BELL
By J.P. Sousa

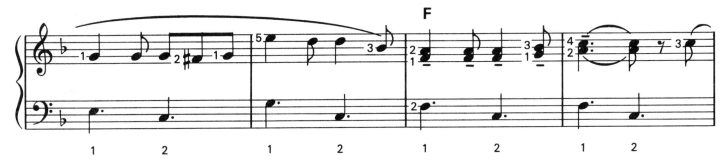

*A piece of music with a strongly emphasized regular meter.

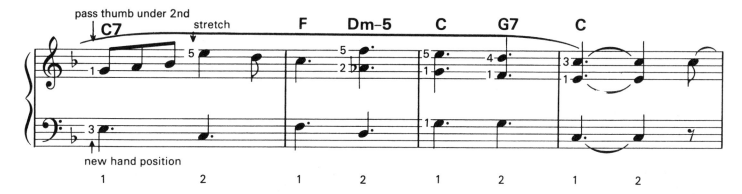

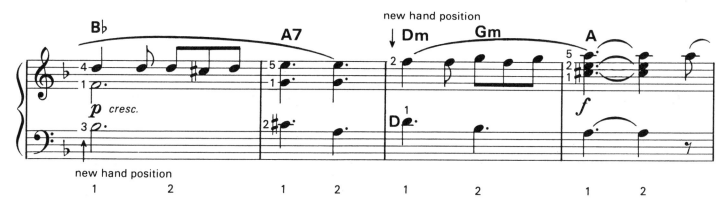

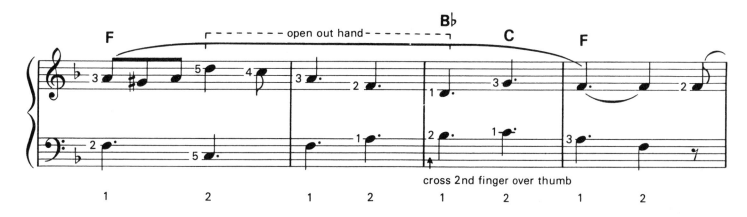

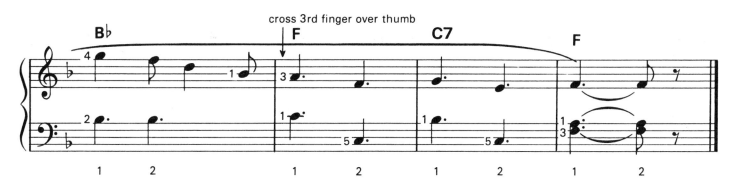

ARPEGGIO (BROKEN CHORD) STYLE FOR LEFT HAND

8

This is another useful accompaniment style, similar in effect to strumming chords on a guitar or banjo.
It is indicated by means of a wavy line:

Play the notes of the chord(s) in rapid succession upwards, rolling your wrist from left to right, yet keeping the wrist relaxed.
Sustain each note on the way up in order to get a rich, full sound.

A SUMMER PLACE

(THEME FROM) A SUMMER PLACE

Words: Mack Discant.
Music: Max Steiner.

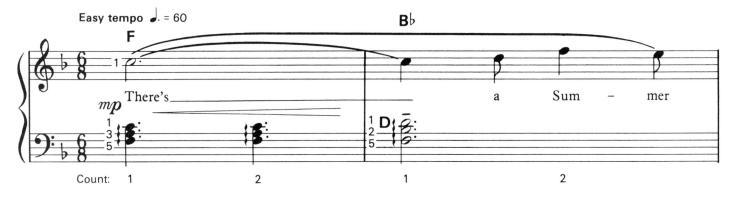

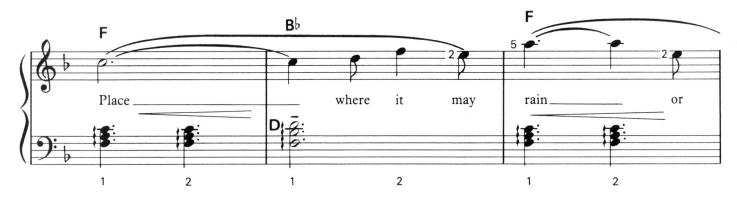

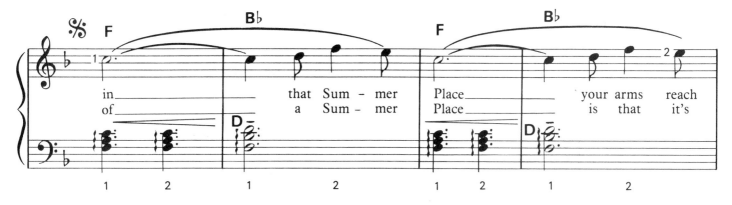

in_____ that Sum - mer Place_____ your arms reach
of_____ a Sum - mer Place_____ is that it's

out_____ to me_____ and my heart_____ is free_____ from all
an - y - where_____ when two peo - ple share_____ all their

care_____ for it knows_____ there are
hopes_____ all their dreams_____ all their

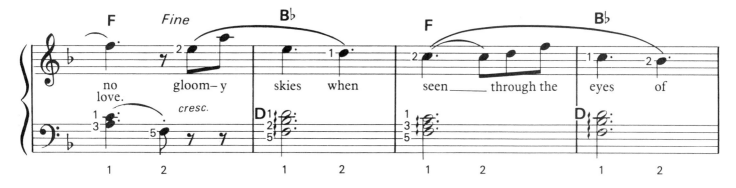

no gloom - y skies when seen_____ through the eyes of
love.

those_____ who are blessed with love. And the sweet se - cret

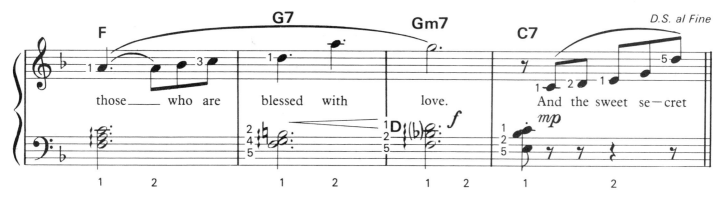

SIXTEENTH NOTES

Written:

Sixteenth notes move twice as fast as eighth notes:

Sixteenth notes are featured in the next piece, *Morning*, by Grieg. To get the basic timing, start by counting the piece in 6:

MORNING

Count:	1	2	3	4	5	6	1	2	3	4	5 and 6 and
(Later):	1		2				1		2		

Later on you will find that the piece will flow better if you count in 2.

MORNING from 'Peer Gynt'
By Edvard Grieg

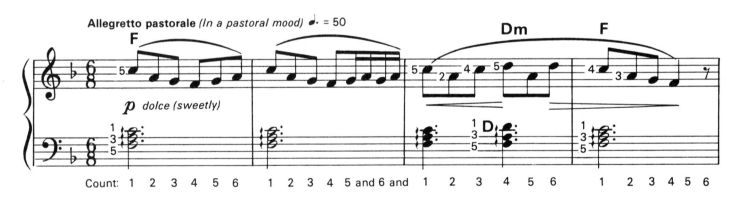

24

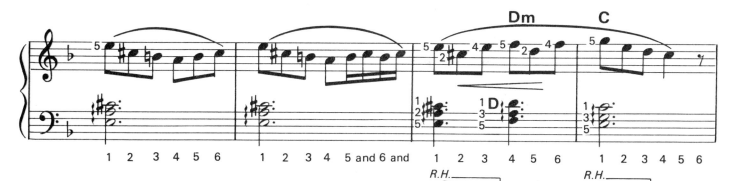

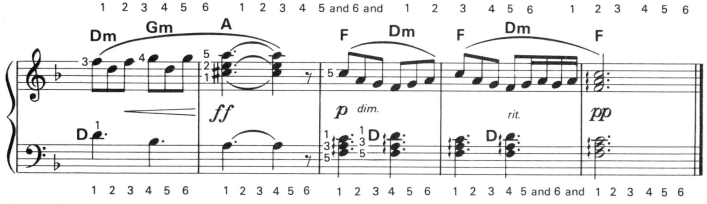

THE WALTZ

10

Although waltzes vary in speed, they are always written in $\frac{3}{4}$ time.

In *Somewhere My Love* (Lara's Theme, from Doctor Zhivago) observe the two-note slurs in the left hand. These will help give the piece "lift".

SOMEWHERE MY LOVE (LARA'S THEME)

Words: Paul Francis Webster. Music: Maurice Jarre

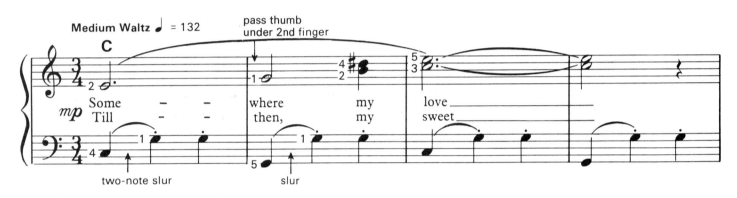

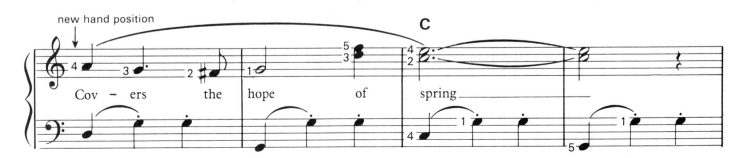

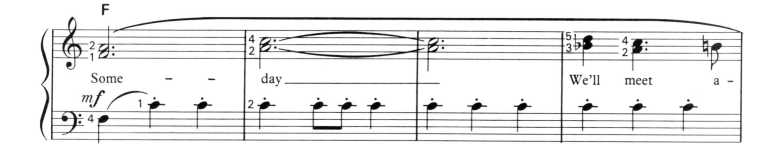

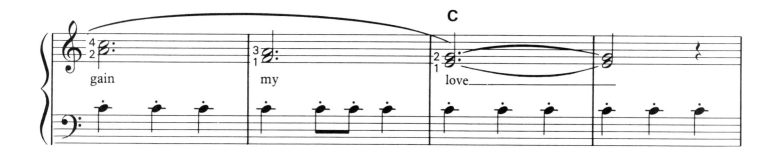

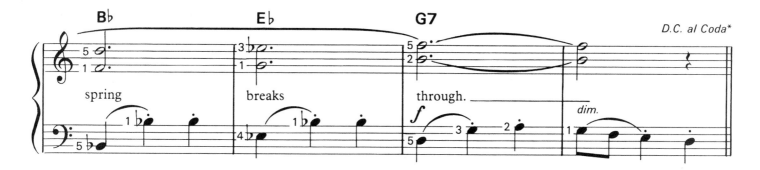

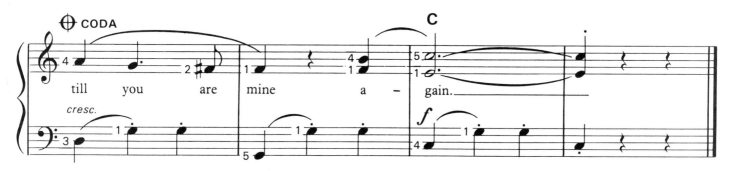

*Da Capo Al Coda: From the beginning to Coda.
Repeat from the beginning of the piece until **to Coda** ⊕

From there jump to the **Coda** (the final section of the piece) and play through to the end .

GRACE NOTES

Grace notes are ornamental notes not included in the basic timing of the bar. They are always written small:

OB LA DI, OB LA DA

grace notes

Play your grace notes as quickly as possible. So, in the above example, hold your half note C for almost its full length. Then slip in the two grace notes just before the quarter note F, which is due on beat 1 of the next bar.

OB-LA-DI, OB-LA-DA

Words & Music: John Lennon and Paul McCartney

Bright ♩ = 100

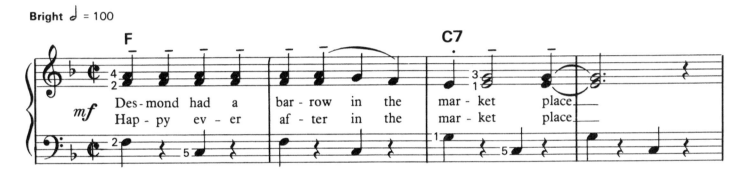

Des - mond had a bar - row in the mar - ket place.
Hap - py ev - er af - ter in the mar - ket place.

Mol - ly is the sin - ger in a band.
Des - mond lets the chil - dren lend a hand.

new hand position

Des - mond says to Mol - ly, "girl I like your face" and Mol - ly
Mol - ly stays at home and does her pret - ty face and in the

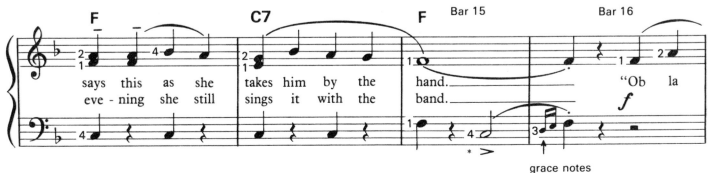

says this as she takes him by the hand.
eve - ning she still sings it with the band.

"Ob la

grace notes

*A strong accent.

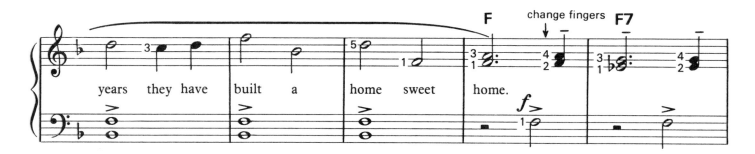

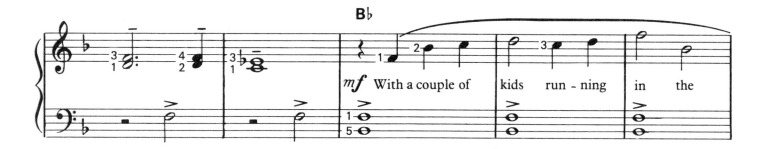

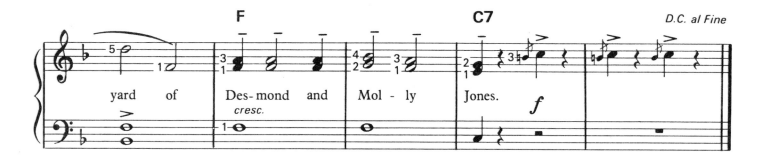

ACCIDENTALS

12

Accidentals are sharps, flats, or naturals which are not expected, because they are not included in the key signature. In the following piece, *Over The Rainbow*, only the F sharp is expected (key of G). All other sharps and flats, and the rather frequent F naturals, are accidentals.

Remember that accidentals only apply to the bar in which they occur. At the next bar everything returns to normal.

OVER THE RAINBOW
Words: E.Y. Harburg. Music: Harold Arlen

true. Some day I'll wish up-on a star and wake up where the clouds are far be-

hind me. Where troub-les melt like lem-on drops, a-

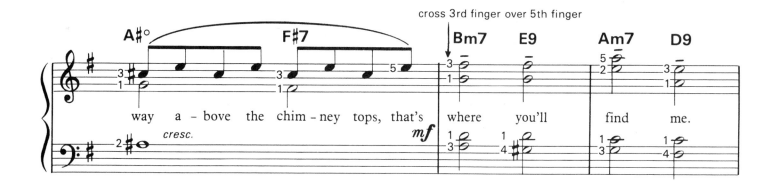

way a-bove the chim-ney tops, that's where you'll find me.

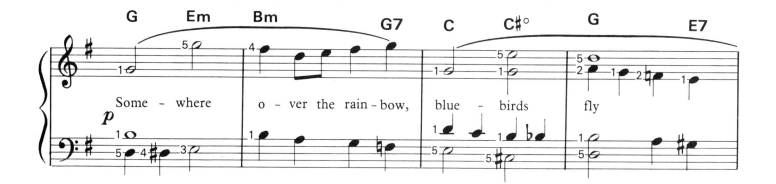

Some-where o-ver the rain-bow, blue-birds fly

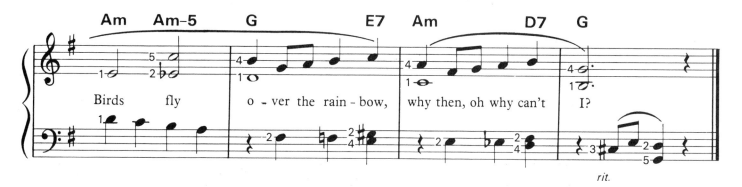

Birds fly o-ver the rain-bow, why then, oh why can't I?

REPEATED NOTES

13 On a number of occasions in your next piece, *Irish Washerwoman*, a note has to be repeated i.e. struck rapidly twice in succession:

IRISH WASHERWOMAN

repeated G

repeated A

(etc)

Be sure to play the first of each pair of repeated notes staccato, otherwise the note will not be ready for use again. You will find 'slur' phrasing, with the hand doing a drop-lift movement each time, a great help in these repeated note passages.

IRISH WASHERWOMAN
Traditional

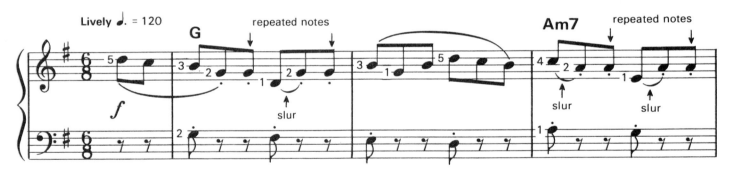

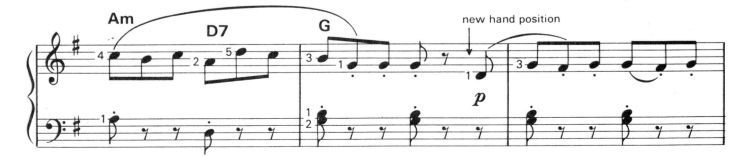

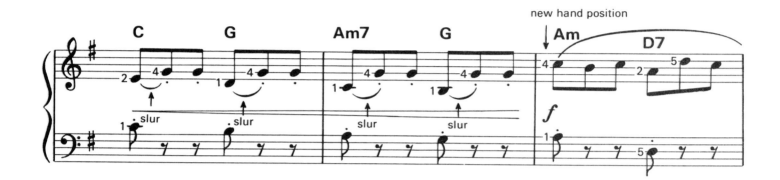

SIXTEENTH NOTES IN $\frac{4}{4}$ TIME

14

In the next piece, *Imagine*, which is written in Common Time ($\frac{4}{4}$) there are a number of sixteenth note fragments mixed in with eighth notes, quarter notes and other time notes.

In such a situation it is probably best, at least in the early stages, to count in eighth notes rather than quarter notes. Each sixteenth note will then have a recognizable place in the count:

IMAGINE

At a later stage, when you have the feel of the timing, you could try counting 4 quarter notes to the bar, rather than 8 eighth notes:

IMAGINE

Words & Music: John Lennon

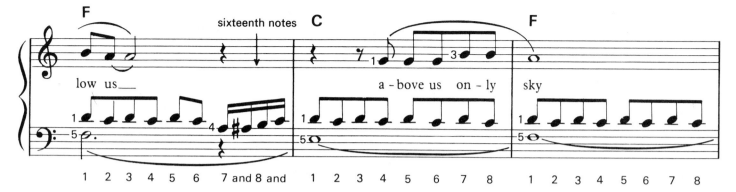

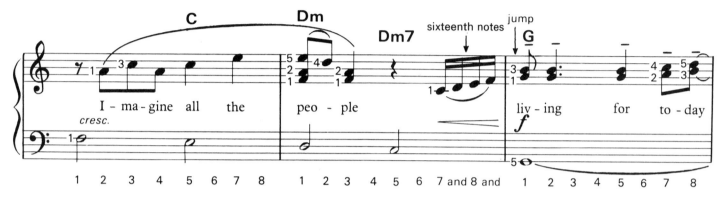

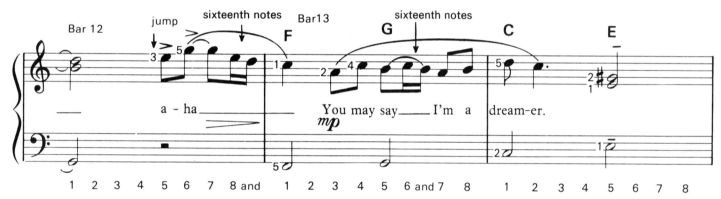

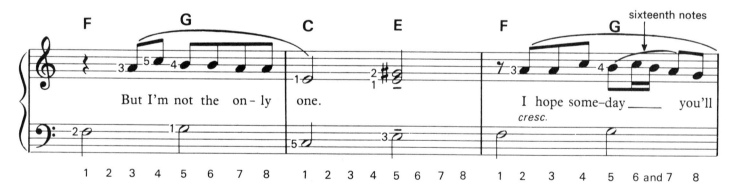

NEW NOTES

15

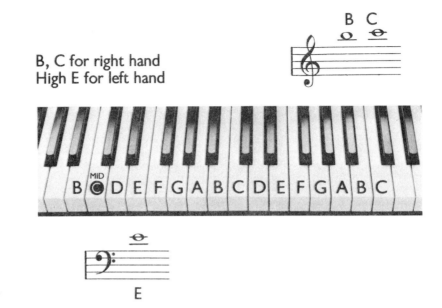

B, C for right hand
High E for left hand

Watch out for these new notes in the next few pieces, the first of which is a charming little piano piece from the Anna Magdalena Notebooks by Bach.

MINUET IN G

By Johann Sebastian Bach

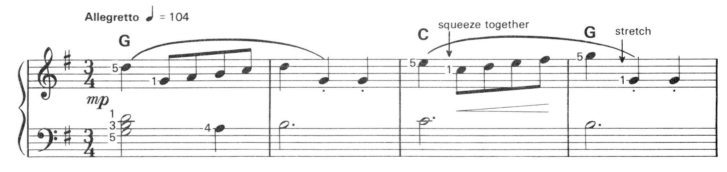

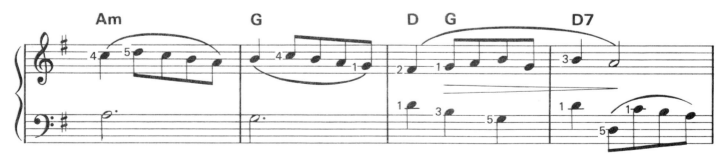

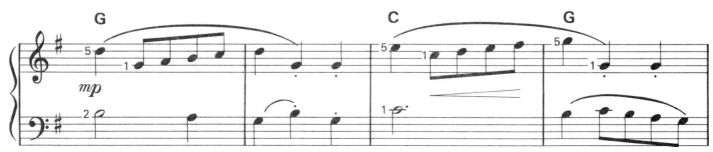

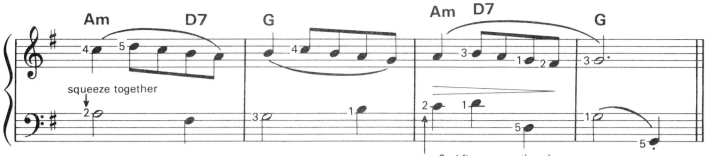

squeeze together

Am D7 G Am D7 G

cross 2nd finger over thumb

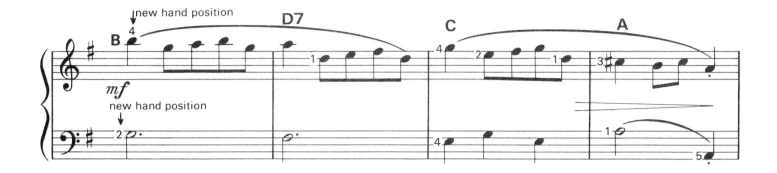

new hand position

B D7 C A

mf

new hand position

pass thumb under 3rd finger

G D A D A D D7

mp

mf

cross 3rd finger over thumb

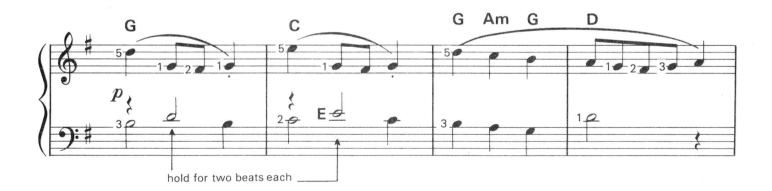

G C G Am G D

p

E

hold for two beats each

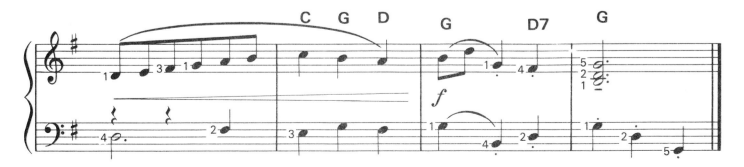

C G D G D7 G

f

TRIPLETS

16

A triplet is a group of 3 notes played in the time of 2.

The most common type of triplet – the eighth note triplet – is written like this:

ARPEGGIO (BROKEN CHORD) **STYLE FOR BOTH HANDS**

In *Amazing Grace* arpeggios work their way upwards through both hands. Start with the lowest left hand note and play rapidly upwards, sustaining each note as you go.

eighth note triplet

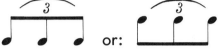 or:

Compare the counting of normal eighth notes and triplet eighth notes:

normal eighth notes

Count: 1   2 and 3   4   and 1 2 3 4

triplet eighth notes

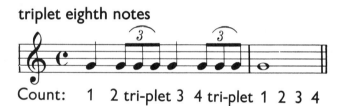

Count: 1   2 tri-plet 3   4 tri-plet 1 2 3 4

You will note that the triplet eighth notes move slightly faster than the normal eighth notes – they have to in order to fit the bar. Be sure to keep your triplet notes regular and even.

Eighth notes triplets appear in your next piece, *Amazing Grace.*

AMAZING GRACE

Traditional

QUARTER NOTE TRIPLET

17 This is another common type of triplet. It consists of 3 quarter notes played in the time of 2:

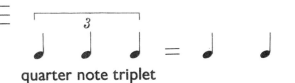

quarter note triplet

Compare the counting of normal quarter notes and triplet quarter notes:

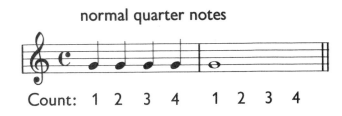

normal quarter notes

Count: 1 2 3 4 1 2 3 4

triplet quarter notes

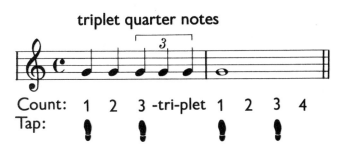

Count: 1 2 3 -tri-plet 1 2 3 4

Tap:

Tap your foot on beats 1 and 3. Start your triplet on beat 3 (a foot-tap) and be ready to play the whole note G on beat 1 of the next bar (the next foot tap). Make sure that your triplet notes in between are regular and even.

The next piece, the theme from the film *Lawrence Of Arabia* will give you plenty of practice in both quarter note and eighth notes triplets.

LAWRENCE OF ARABIA

Words & Music: Maurice Jarre.

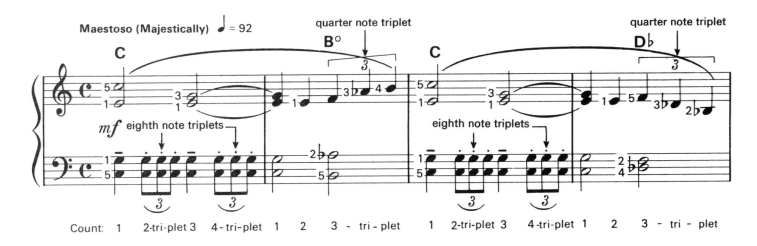

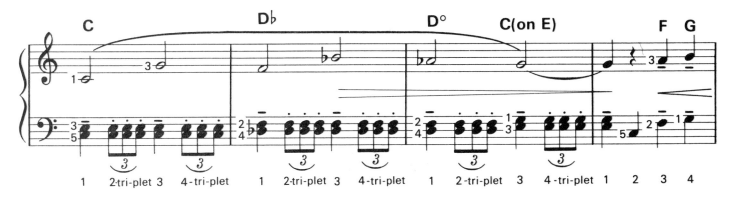

MORE LEFT HAND MELODY PLAYING

18

For much of the next piece, *Getting To Know You*, the melody is in the left hand. Adjust the sound balance between the two hands so that the left hand predominates. You will find that careful attention to the phrasing marks (staccato, legato, and so on) will also help bring out the melody.

Note the eighth note triplets in *Getting To Know You*.

GETTING TO KNOW YOU
FROM 'THE KING AND I'

Words: Oscar Hammerstein II. Music: Richard Rodgers

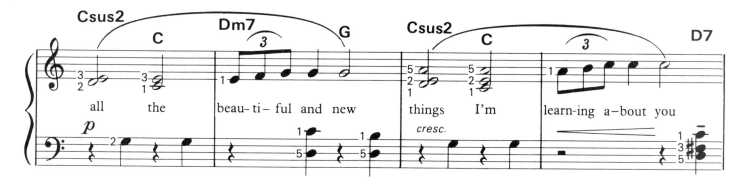

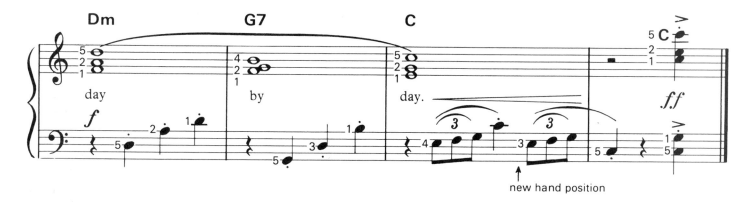

DOTTED EIGHTH NOTE

19 As you learned in Book Two, (p.38), a dot after a note increases its length by one-half. So, a dotted eighth note is equal to 1½ eighth notes or 3 sixteenth notes:

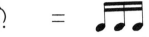

dotted eighth note   3 sixteenth notes

A dotted eighth rest, a silence equal to one dotted eighth note, is written like this:

ɣ· dotted eighth note rest

A dotted eighth note usually pairs up with a sixteenth note, since together they make up 1 quarter note beat:

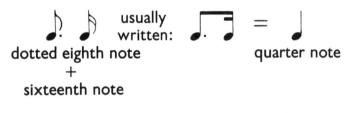

dotted eighth note
+
sixteenth note

The general effect of a passage like:

is of eighth notes with a "lilt."

Use the phrase **humpty dumpty** as a guide to this rhythm:

say: Hump-ty Dump-ty   Hump-ty Dump-ty
        ▲   ▲   ▲   ▲
      stress   stress   stress   stress

These uneven types of rhythms are often called 'dotted rhythms'.

Look out for dotted rhythms in the next three pieces.

YELLOW SUBMARINE

Words & Music: John Lennon and Paul McCartney

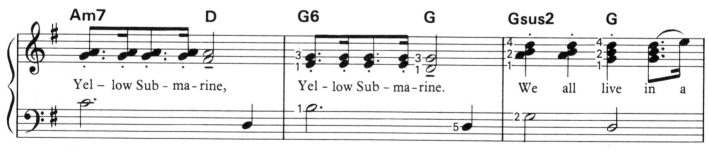

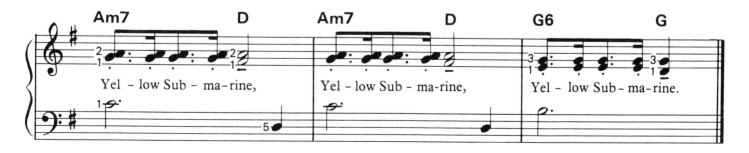

SWING

20

Swing, a jazz style developed in the 1930's, is still popular today.

One of the main characteristics of swing is its use of lilting dotted rhythms. However, in Swing a phrase like:

say: hump-ty   dump-ty

↑ stress and hold back

would not be taken literally, but played in

a more relaxed manner, like this:

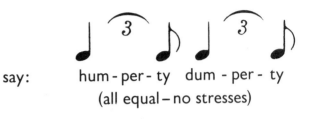

say: hum-per-ty   dum-per-ty
(all equal – no stresses)

You will be playing these sorts of dotted rhythms in *Raindrops Keep Fallin' On My Head*, a modern tune written in the Swing idiom.

RAINDROPS KEEP FALLIN' ON MY HEAD

Words: Hal David. Music: Burt Bacharach

LAST WORD

So we come to the end of Book Three of *The Complete Piano Player*.

You are now familiar with the middle range of the piano, and Book Three has introduced you to some quite advanced timings and rhythm patterns.

In Book Four you will be:
- Learning more new notes
- Adding a little syncopation
- Playing in new keys
- Using the piano pedals
- Discovering new piano techniques

Till then your last song in this book is:

THE WONDER OF YOU

Words & Music: Baker Knight

THE COMPLETE PIANO PLAYER
BOOK 4

'By the end of this book your playing will
be even more colorful and varied,
and you will be playing 22 popular songs,
including: *Don't Cry For Me Argentina,
Just The Way You Are,
The Sound Of Silence,* and *My Way.'*

Kenneth Baker

Amsco Publications
New York/London/Sydney

Exclusive Distributors:
Music Sales Corporation
257 Park Avenue South, New York, NY 10010, USA

This book Copyright © 1984 and 1985 by
Amsco Publications
Order No. AM 39645
International Standard Book Number: 0.8256.2439.8

Designed by Howard Brown
Photography by Peter Wood
Arranged by Kenneth Baker

Printed in the United States of America by
Vicks Lithograph and Printing Corporation

CONTENTS

ABOUT THIS BOOK

Book Four takes you a giant step along your road to becoming the complete piano player.

It introduces you to the piano pedals, and you will be delighted at how much color the Sustaining Pedal will add to your playing.

Your study of 'syncopation' begins here too, and you will learn several great syncopated numbers guaranteed to set the foot tapping.

Because it is important, for the sake of contrast, to play in a number of different keys, you will learn five new ones– including three 'minor' keys.

There are also some new piano techniques which will improve your playing, such as playing in octaves with the right hand, and 'filling in' with the left hand.

As usual all lessons are based on well known songs made famous by great artists, or tuneful classical compositions. By the end of the book you will have twenty-two exciting new solos to add to your repertoire.

FIVE NEW NOTES FOR LEFT HAND

Here are some important new notes for you to learn:

Low C, D and E
High F and F Sharp

All for left hand

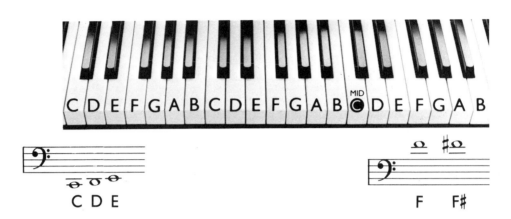

C D E

F F#

YOUNGER THAN SPRINGTIME
(FROM 'SOUTH PACIFIC')
Words: Oscar Hammerstein II. Music: Richard Rodgers

Con espressione ♩ = 60

Young – er than Spring – time
Gay – er than laugh – ter
are you
are you
Soft – er than star – light
Sweet – er than mu – sic

are you,
are you,
Warm – er than winds of
An – gel and lov – er,
June are the gen – tle
heav – en and earth are

lips you
you to
gave me
me. And when your

6

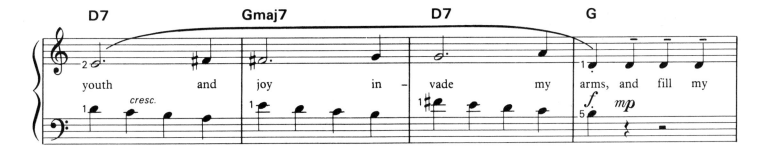

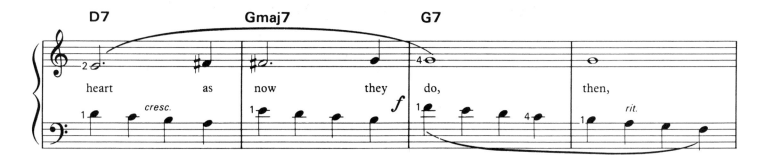

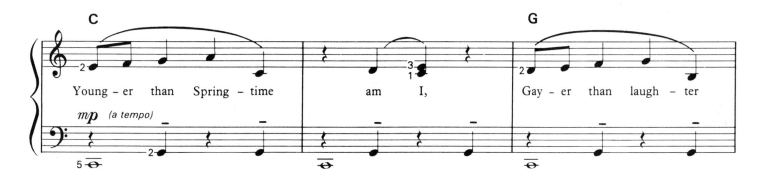

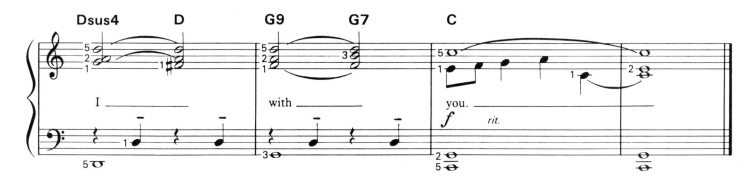

Look out for the new left hand low notes
in the following piece.

HELLO YOUNG LOVERS
(FROM 'THE KING AND I')
Words: Oscar Hammerstein II. Music: Richard Rodgers

Brightly ♩ = 160

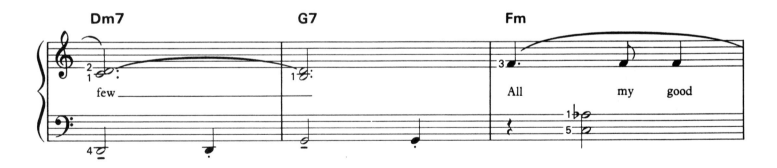

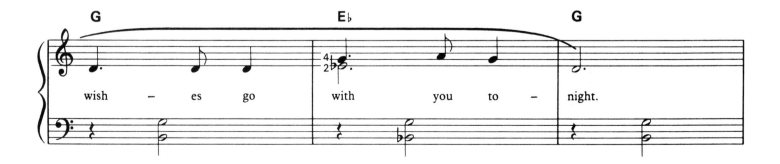

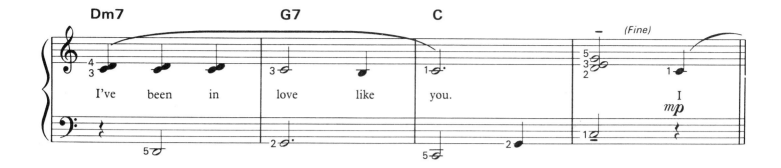

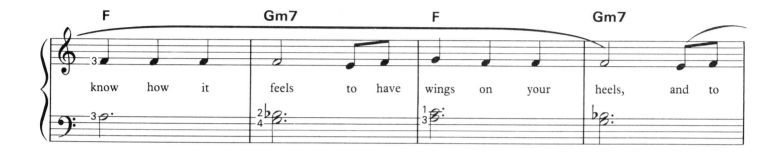

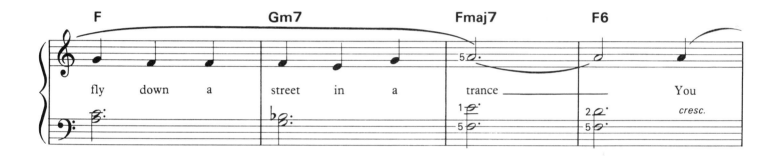

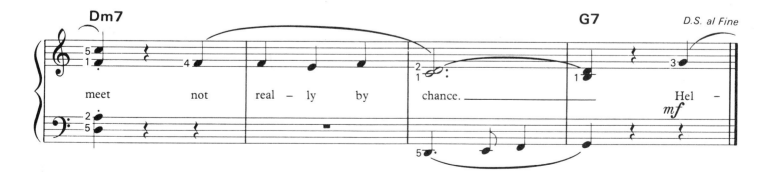

THREE NEW NOTES FOR RIGHT HAND

2

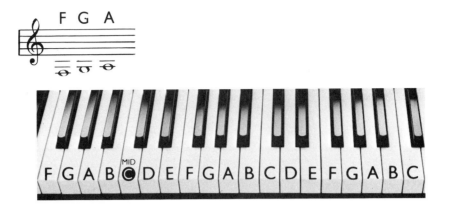

ISN'T SHE LOVELY
Words & Music: Stevie Wonder

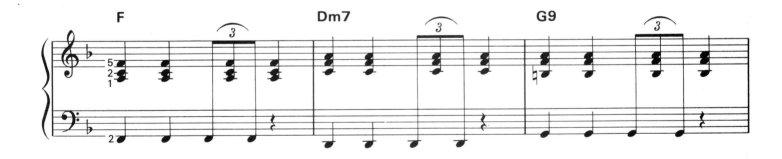

Is - n't she love - ly

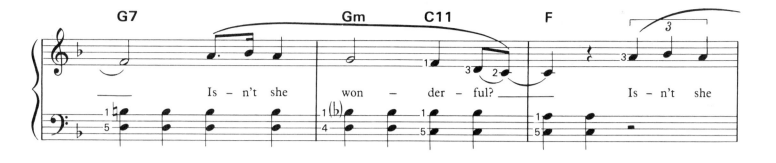

Is-n't she won - der - ful? Is-n't she

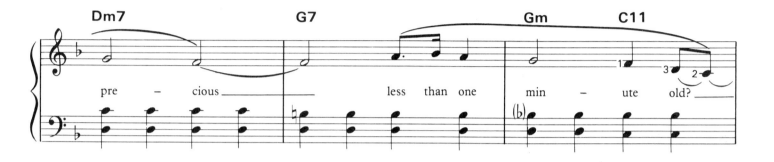

pre - cious _____ less than one min - ute old? _____

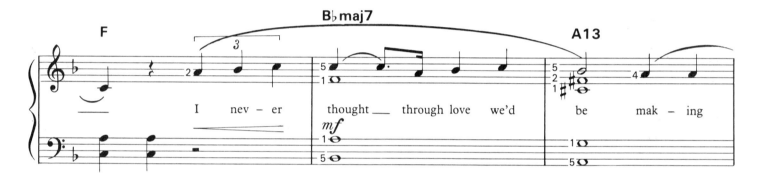

I nev - er thought _____ through love we'd be mak - ing

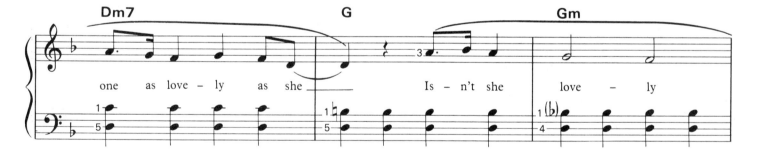

one as love - ly as she _____ Is - n't she love - ly

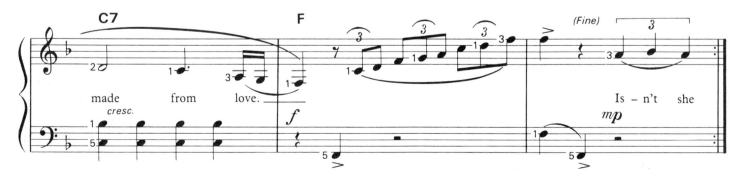

made from love. Is-n't she

Look out for the new right hand notes in
the following piece.

MARCH OF THE SIAMESE CHILDREN
(FROM 'THE KING AND I')

By Richard Rodgers

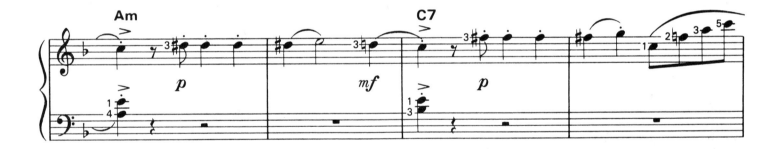

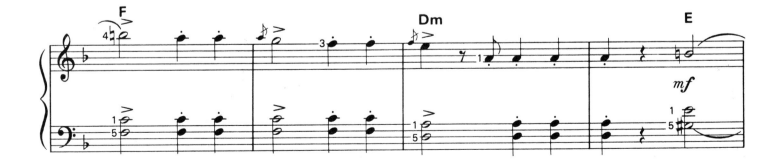

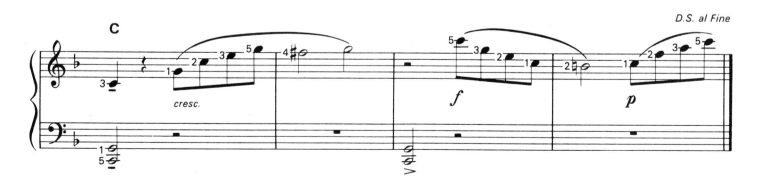

THE PEDALS ON THE PIANO

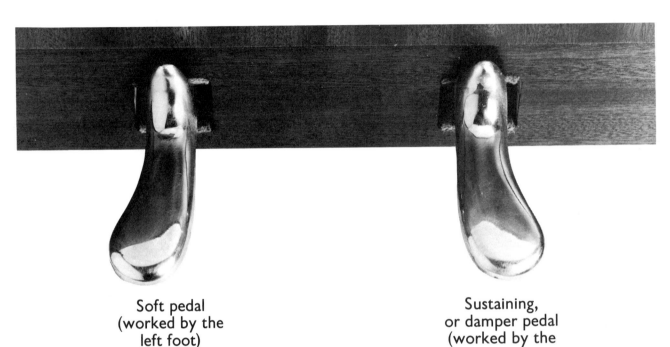

Soft pedal
(worked by the
left foot)

Sustaining,
or damper pedal
(worked by the
right foot)

Soft Pedal
This pedal produces a softer, lighter tone than usual. It is usually indicated in music by the words 'una corda'.

Sustaining, or damper pedal
This pedal lifts the dampers from the strings. This causes the notes played to ring on after the fingers have been lifted from the keys.

The sustaining pedal is the more important of the two pedals. There are several ways of indicating its use. The method we shall use for the moment is:

meaning: pedal down   (hold pedal down)   pedal up

meaning: pedal down   (hold pedal down)   change pedal   (hold pedal down)

(i.e. lift fully then press down again immediately)

The sustaining pedal has two main functions:

1. To combine the notes of a chord:

pedal down   (hold pedal down throughout)   pedal up

2. To link notes in cases where it would be impossible to do so using the fingers alone:

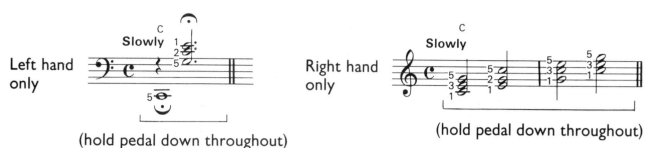

Left hand only

(hold pedal down throughout)

Right hand only

(hold pedal down throughout)

When the harmonies of a piece change it is usual to change the sustaining pedal also:

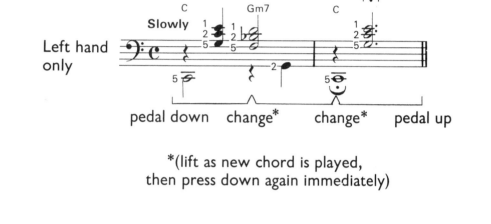

Left hand only

pedal down   change*   change*   pedal up

*(lift as new chord is played,
then press down again immediately)

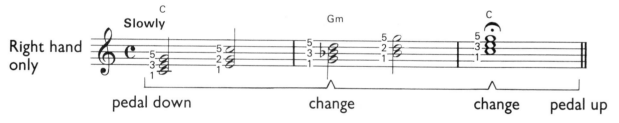

Right hand only

pedal down   change   change   pedal up

PEDAL CHANGING EXERCISE

Using **second finger only,** plus pedal, play the scale below so that it sounds completely 'legato' (connected).

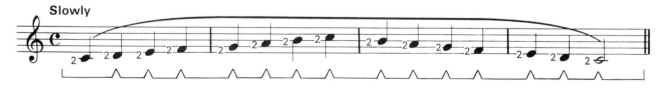

Practice this exercise until you can perform perfect pedal changes.

Here now are four pieces which will give you practice in using the sustaining pedal. **Practice each piece first without the pedal.** Add the pedal as you become more familiar with the notes. Observe all pedal markings carefully. When making a pedal 'change' note that as the fingers go 'down' (on the new note(s)) the pedal comes 'up'. (It will then go immediately down again).

SCARBOROUGH FAIR

Traditional

THE SOUND OF SILENCE

Words & Music: Paul Simon

*Although the harmony here does not require a change of pedal, the melody does.

BROKEN CHORD STYLE FOR LEFT HAND

4

In this style the left hand provides a nice flowing accompaniment by moving up and down the notes of the chord. The style is greatly enhanced by the use of the sustaining pedal, since this causes the single notes to build into full chords.

This style is different from the 'arpeggio (broken chord) style' for left hand, first used in Book Three, p.22. In that earlier style the left hand simply split the notes of the chord rapidly upwards, and involved no specific timing. Here there is a rhythm pattern present.

MY WAY

Original French Lyrics: Gilles Thibault.
Words: Paul Anka.
Music: J. Revaux and C. Francois.

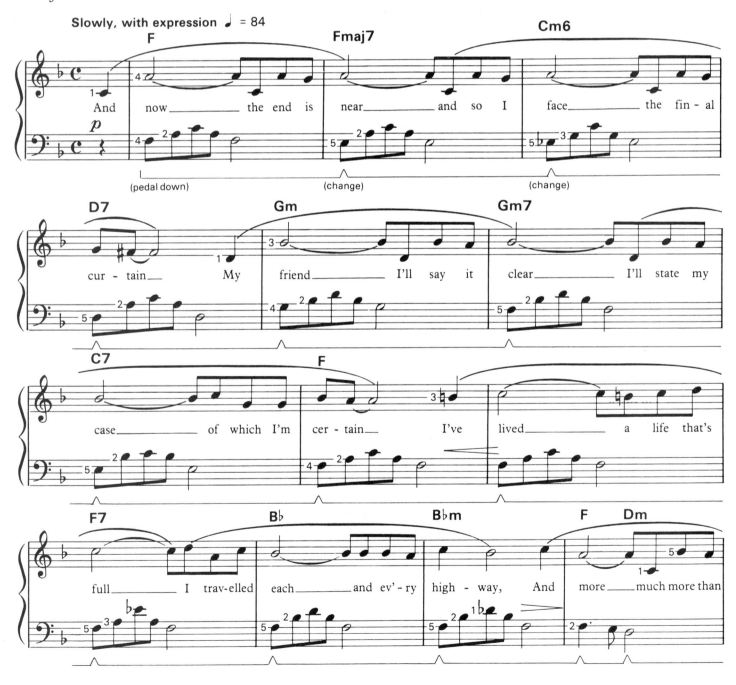

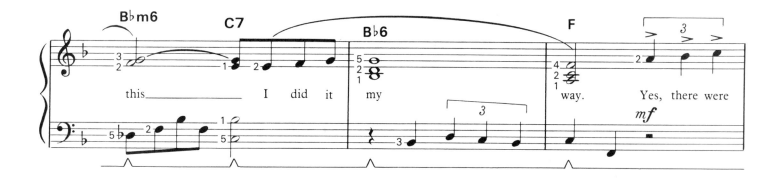

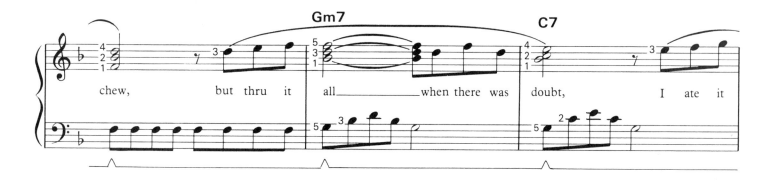

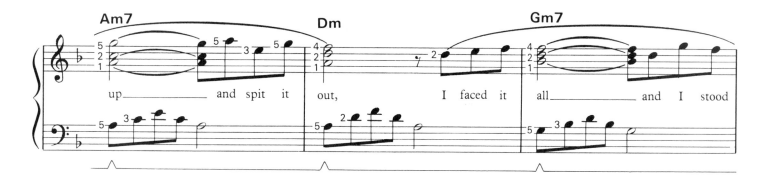

19

Before playing the next piece turn back
to Book Three, p.16, and read about
⁶⁄₈ Time again.

(THEME FROM) VIOLIN CONCERTO (SLOW MOVEMENT)

By Felix Mendelssohn

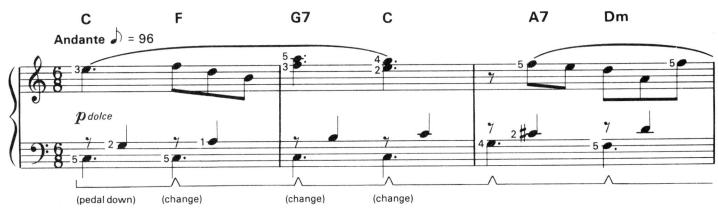

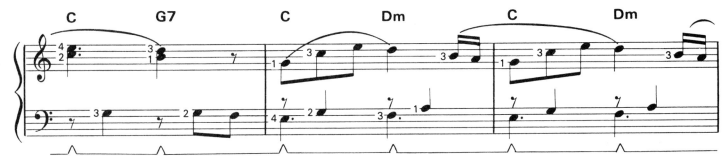

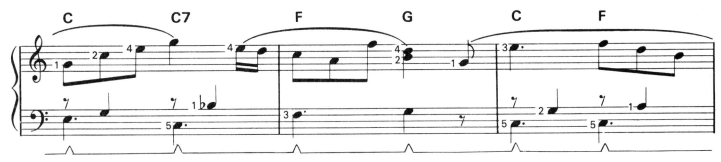

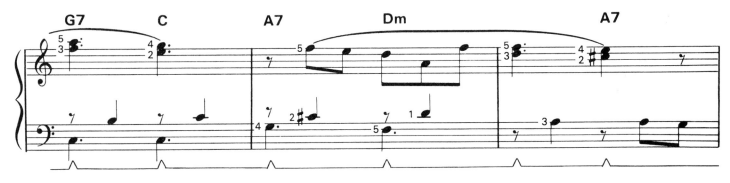

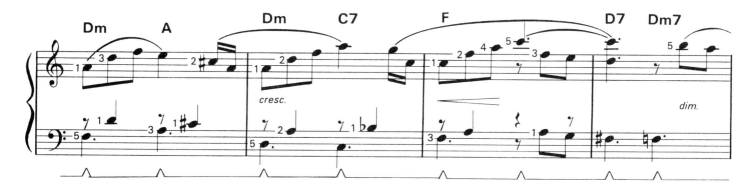

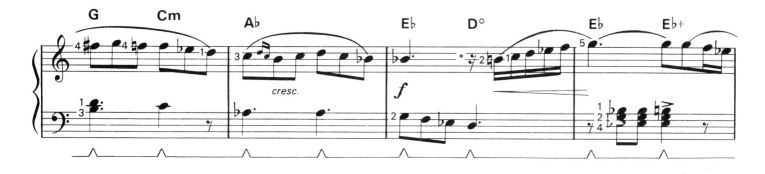

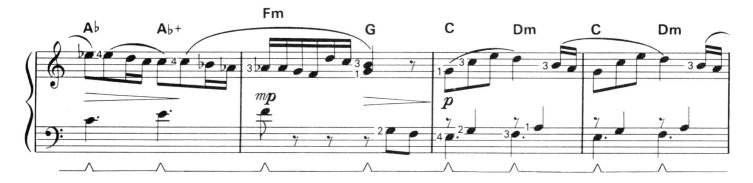

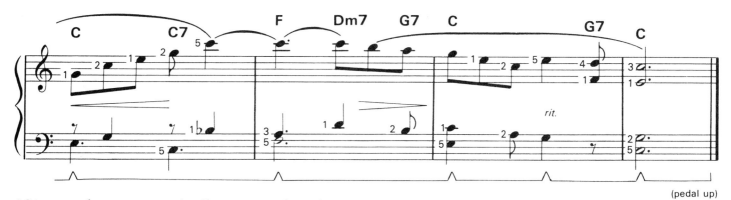

(pedal up)

*Sixteenth note rest (a silence equal to the value of one sixteenth note).

KEY OF B FLAT

5

The 'Key of B flat (major)' is derived from the 'Scale of B flat (major)', which requires two black notes: B flat and E flat:

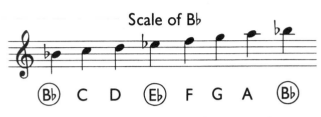

Scale of Bb

(Bb) C D (Eb) F G A (Bb)

Pieces using this scale predominantly are said to be in the 'key of B flat'.

The 'Key signature' for the Key of Bb is:-

Key of Bb

B Flat, E Flat

B Flat, E Flat

When you are in this Key you must remember to play all B's and E's (wherever they might fall on the keyboard) as B flats and E flats.

THE FOOL ON THE HILL

Words & Music: John Lennon and Paul McCartney

Con moto (with movement) ♩ = 108

Bbmaj7   Cm7

Day af-ter day   a - lone on a hill

mp

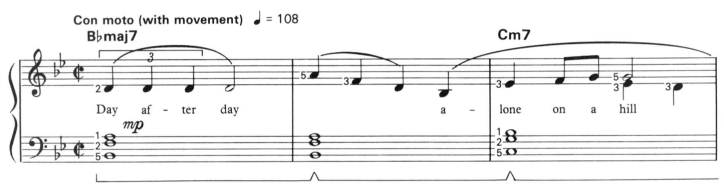

F7   Bbmaj7   Bb6

The man with the fool – ish grin is keep – ing

Cm7   F7   Cm7

per – fect – ly still   But no – bo – dy wants to

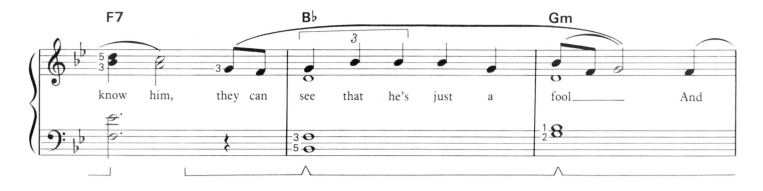

know him, they can see that he's just a fool_____ And

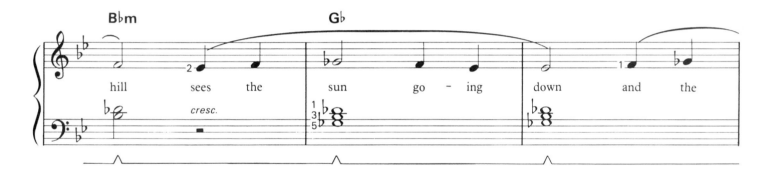

he nev - er gives an an - swer, but the fool_____ on the

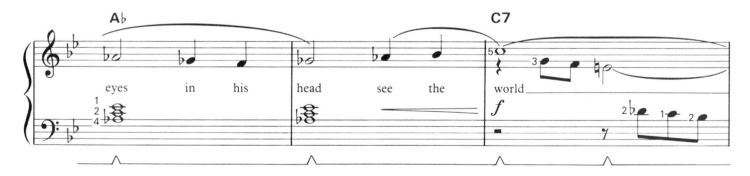

hill sees the sun go - ing down and the

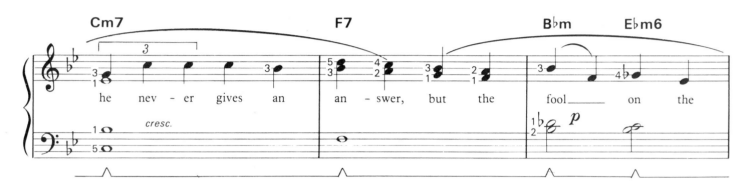

eyes in his head see the world_____

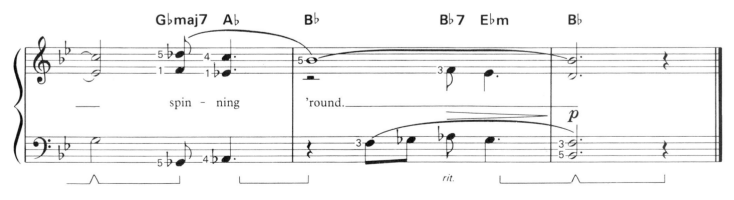

_____ spin - ning 'round._____

VERSE AND CHORUS

6

Mockin' Bird Hill is divided into two main sections: the 'verse' and the 'chorus'. The Verse section of a song usually contains the bulk of the narrative and is sung by a solo singer. The Chorus (the main and usually the best known section of a song) is the part where the audience joins in.

You will get a crisper effect from this piece if you do not use the sustaining pedal.

Before you play *Mockin' Bird Hill* turn back to Book Three, p.18, and re-read about 'two-note slurs'.

MOCKIN' BIRD HILL
Words & Music: Vaughn Horton

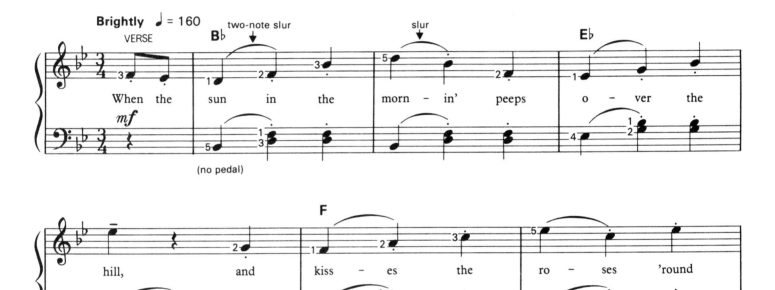

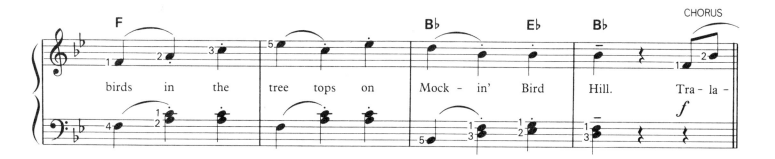

birds in the tree tops on Mock-in' Bird Hill. Tra-la-

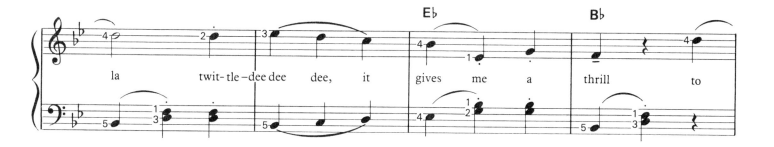

la twit-tle-dee dee dee, it gives me a thrill to

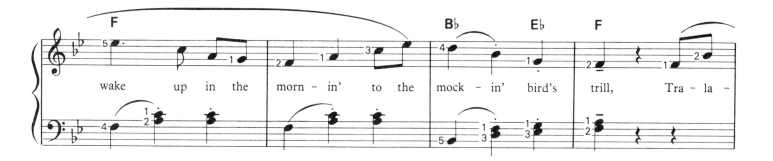

wake up in the morn-in' to the mock-in' bird's trill, Tra-la-

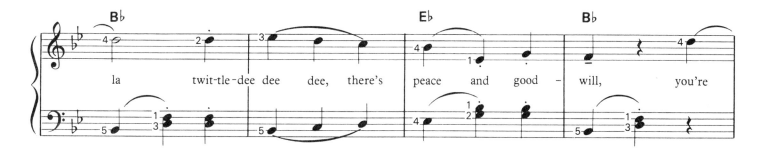

la twit-tle-dee dee dee, there's peace and good-will, you're

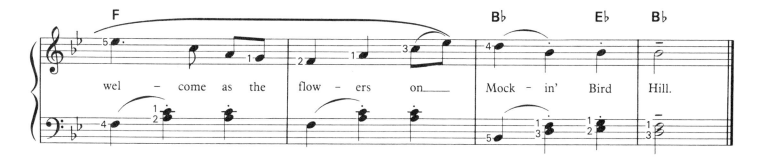

wel-come as the flow-ers on_____ Mock-in' Bird Hill.

SYNCOPATION

7

When an important, accented note is played just before, or just after a main beat, rather than on it, the effect is called 'syncopation'.

For example:

Example 1

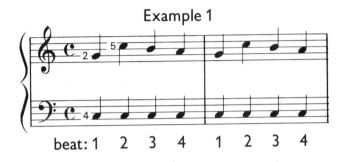

beat: 1 2 3 4 1 2 3 4

No syncopation (each melody note is played on a main beat).

Example 2   Bar 2

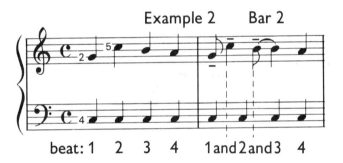

beat: 1 2 3 4 1 and 2 and 3 4

Syncopation in Bar 2 (Melody notes 'C' and 'B' play **in between** main beats).

Play the second example through several times. The repeated left hand 'C's' will give you the main beats. Keep the left hand rock-steady throughout.

The above is a simplified version of the start of *Peacherine Rag*. Here now are these same two bars as you will actually play them:

Example 3 Peacherine Rag

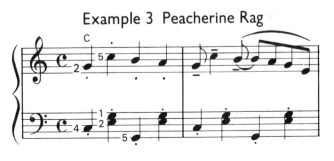

beat: 1 2 3 4 1 and 2 and 3 and 4 and

Play Example 3 through many times to get the feel of the syncopation. Keep the left hand rock-steady and play the right hand melody notes with, and in between, the left hand notes as required.

PEACHERINE RAG

By Scott Joplin

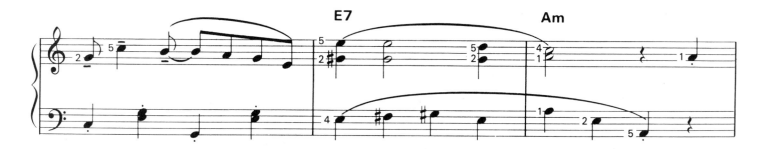

Here's a famous modern piece which uses syncopation: *The Fifty-Ninth Street Bridge Song,* by Paul Simon.

Notice the Swing-style 'dotted rhythms' (see Book Three, p.46) which help give the piece a nice lilt.

I have arrowed the first seven syncopated notes for you. Try to find the others for yourself (there are eighteen more). As in *'Peacherine Rag',* keep your left hand rock-steady throughout.

THE FIFTY-NINTH STREET BRIDGE SONG
(FEELIN' GROOVY)

Words & Music: Paul Simon

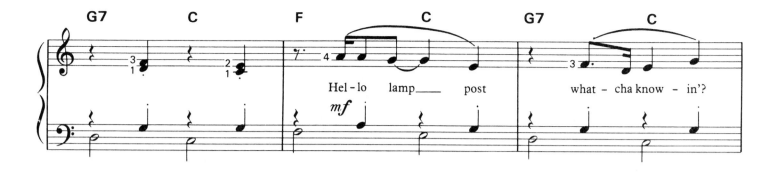

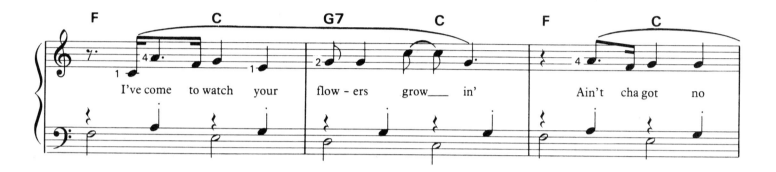

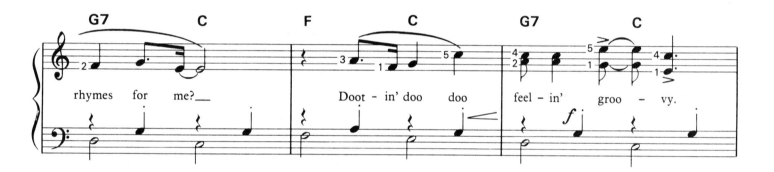

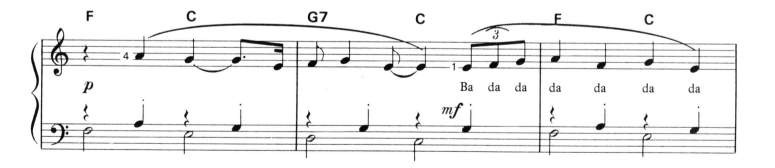

Latin American style tunes use
syncopation too, as can be seen in this
charming Bossa Nova* called 'Little Boat'.

Since the left hand does not play on
every beat in this piece you will have to
maintain a strong rhythm in your head!

O BARQUINHO (LITTLE BOAT)

Music: Roberto Menescal. Original Words: Ronaldo Boscoli. English Lyric: Buddy Kaye

*A Latin-American dance rhythm.

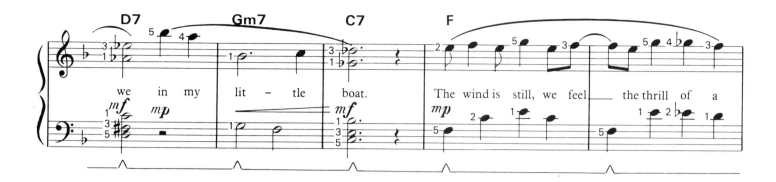

we in my lit—tle boat. The wind is still, we feel___ the thrill of a

voy-age heav-en bound, tho we on–ly drift a-round. Warmed by the sun, two hearts___

as one beat–ing with en-chant-ed bliss, melt-ing in each oth-er's kiss. When day – light ends and sly–

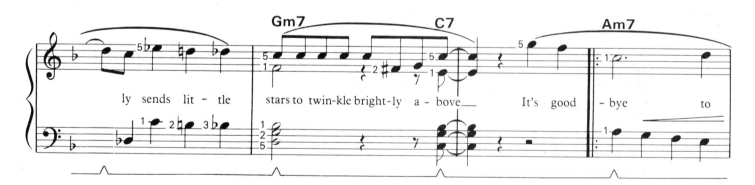

ly sends lit – tle stars to twin-kle bright-ly a - bove___ It's good – bye to

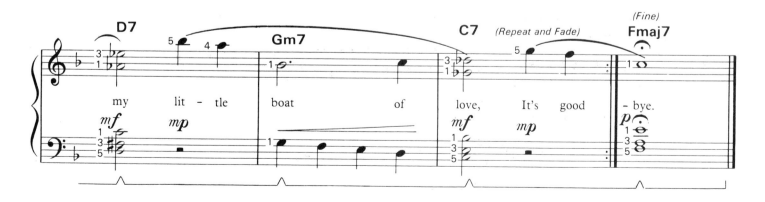

my lit – tle boat of love, It's good – bye.

When I'm Sixty-four is an example of
syncopation from The Beatles songbook.

WHEN I'M 64

(Words & Music: John Lennon and Paul McCartney)

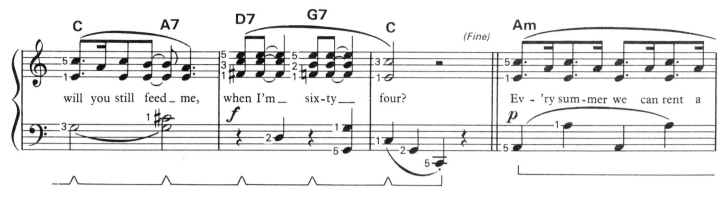

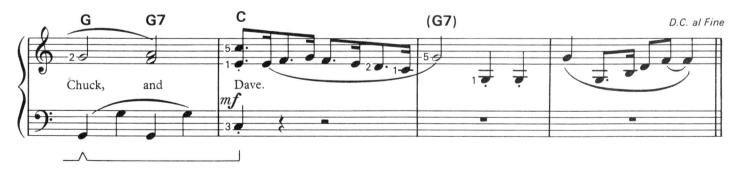

KEY OF D

The 'Key of D (major)' is derived from the 'Scale of D (major)', which requires two black notes: F sharp and C sharp:

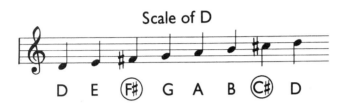

Scale of D

D E (F#) G A B (C#) D

The Key signature is therefore:

Key of D

F sharp, C sharp

F sharp, C sharp

When you are in this Key you must remember to play all F's and C's (wherever they might fall on the keyboard) as F sharps and C sharps.

Notice the Left Hand accompaniment 'patterns' in the chorus of the following piece.

DON'T CRY FOR ME ARGENTINA

Music: Andrew Lloyd Webber. Lyrics: Tim Rice

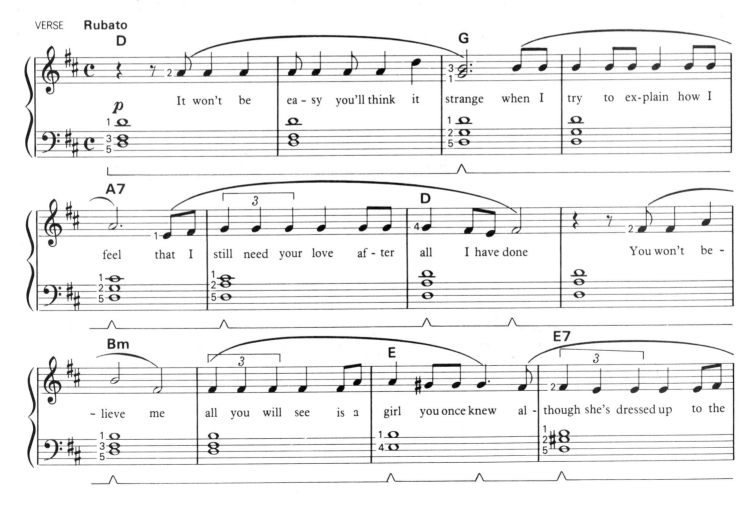

*A popular dance rhythm of African and
Latin-American origin.

KEY OF D MINOR

9

The Key of D Minor is derived from the Scale of D Minor, which requires one black note: B flat:

Scale of D Minor (Natural)

D E F G A (B♭) C D

The key signature is therefore:

Key of D Minor

B flat

This is the same key signature as F Major:-

Key of F (Major)

B flat

Since they share the same key signature, these two keys are said to be 'related':

D Minor is the Relative Minor of F Major

F Major is the Relative Major of D Minor

Quite often in the key of D Minor you will come across a C 'sharp' or a B 'natural'. Neither of these notes appears in the scale given above. These variations occur because there are two other types of D Minor scale in common use which actually use C sharp and B natural:

Scale of D Minor (Harmonic)

D E F G A (B♭) (C♯) D

Scale of D Minor (Melodic)

D E F G A (B) (C♯) D

When in the key of D Minor remember:

1. You must play all B's (wherever they might fall on the keyboard) as B flats.

2. Look out for occasional C sharps and B naturals (they will be marked as they occur).

OCTAVES IN THE RIGHT HAND

10

This is a most important piano technique which will make your playing sound fuller and more professional.

First practise playing a scale (the scale of C will do) with your right hand to get the feeling of 'octaves' (a distance of eight notes):

Scale of C

(Repeat ad lib)

Try other scales similarly.

Next go over some of the easier pieces in the previous books, playing your right hand in octaves throughout.

Note: if the size of your hand allows, finger all black note octaves: $\frac{4}{1}$ rather than: $\frac{5}{1}$. This makes for smoother playing.

The next piece: '*The Green Leaves Of Summer*' is in the key of D Minor.

In the first part your left hand will be using a technique which you have seen before: 'chord pyramids' (see Book Three, p.6).

In the second part your right hand will play the melody in 'octaves'. Since this involves jumping about you will need to use the sustaining pedal to make this section sound 'legato'.

THE GREEN LEAVES OF SUMMER

Words: Paul Francis Webster. Music: Dimitri Tiomkin

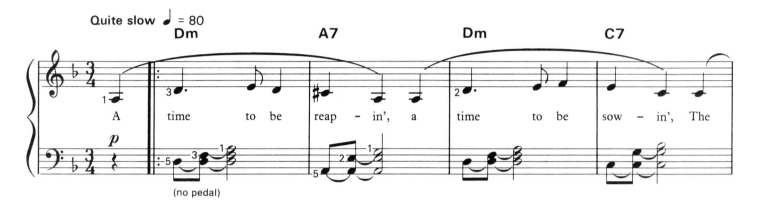

A time to be reap – in', a time to be sow – in', The

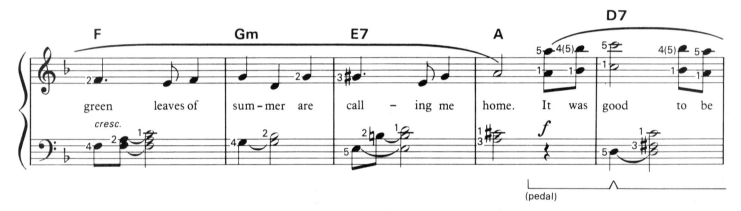

green leaves of sum – mer are call – ing me home. It was good to be

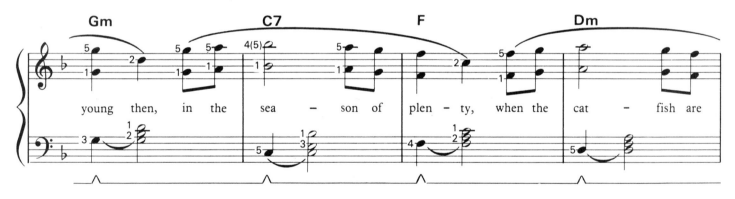

young then, in the sea – son of plen – ty, when the cat – fish are

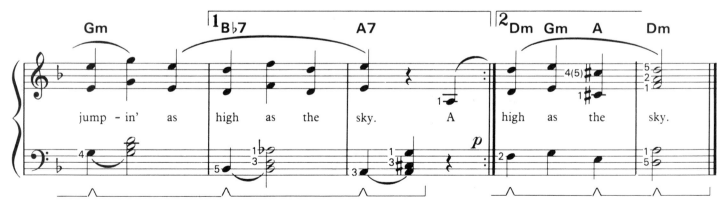

jump – in' as high as the sky. A high as the sky.

'Hava Nagila' (in the key of D minor) will give you further practice in right hand octaves.

If you have a large hand, finger the 'black note' octaves $\frac{4}{1}$: if not you will have to finger all octaves $\frac{5}{1}$.

HAVA NAGILA
Traditional

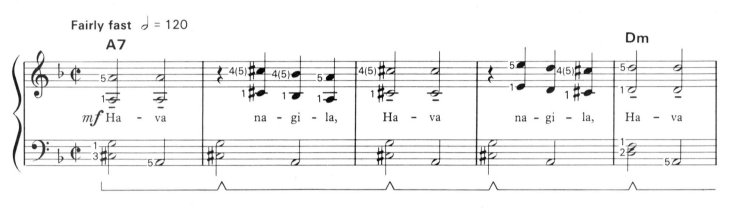

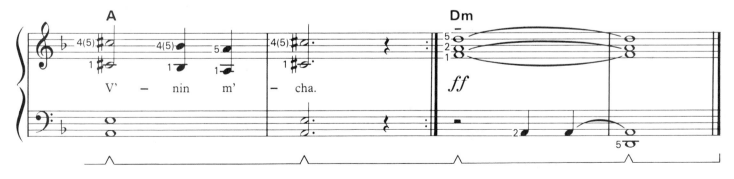

KEY OF E MINOR

E Minor is the 'Relative Minor' of G Major, both keys requiring one sharp: F sharp:

The 'accidentals'* likely to occur in the Key of E Minor (due to other forms of the E Minor Scale) are: D# and C#

MY FAVORITE THINGS
(FROM 'THE SOUND OF MUSIC')

Words: Oscar Hammerstein II. Music: Richard Rodgers

*Temporary sharps, flats, or naturals.

40

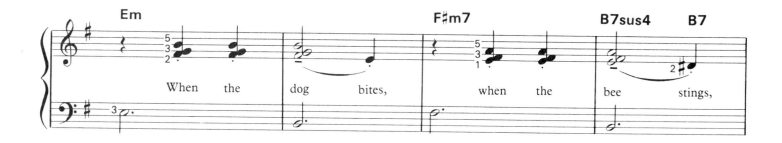

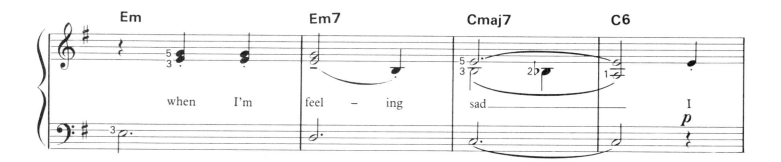

ALTERNATIVE PEDAL MARKING

12 An alternative and simpler method of indicating the sustaining pedal will be used from now on:

P means 'apply' or 'change' the pedal, the equivalent of: ⎿_____⏌ or: ⎿_____⋀ * means 'lift' the Pedal.

LEFT HAND FILLS

13 In *'Laura'* your left hand will be playing 'fills' or 'fill-ins'. These are short melodic fragments which fill in the 'dead spots' in the right hand part and help keep the piece moving. Play all your fills 'legato' and with expression.

LAURA
Words: Johnny Mercer. Music: David Raksin

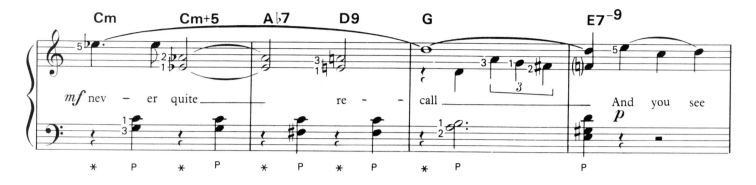

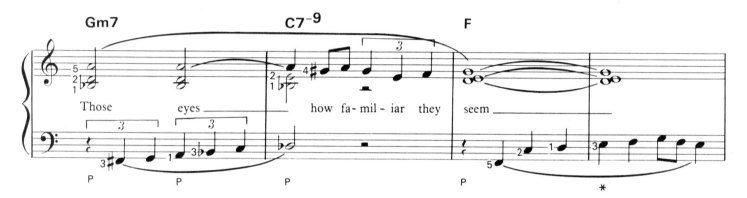

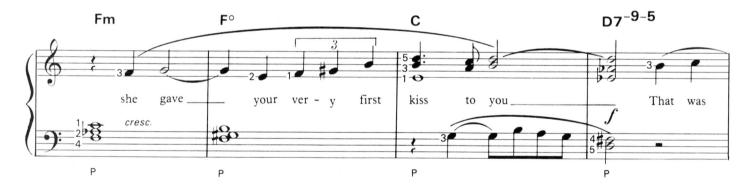

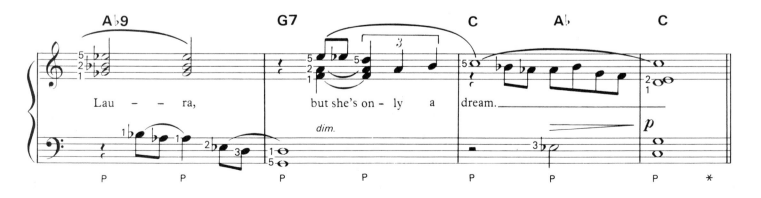

BOSSA NOVA RHYTHM PATTERN

14 In the next piece you play a simple, but effective Bossa Nova rhythm pattern in your left hand:

count: 1   2 and 3   4

The pattern begins in Bar 5 and continues through most of the first part of the song.

JUST THE WAY YOU ARE
Words & Music: Billy Joel

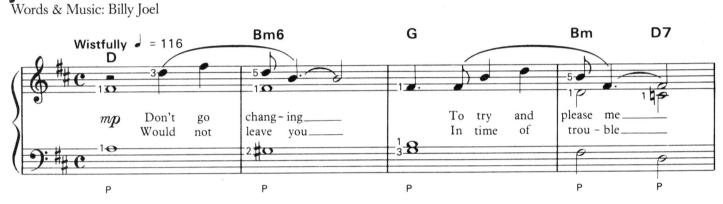

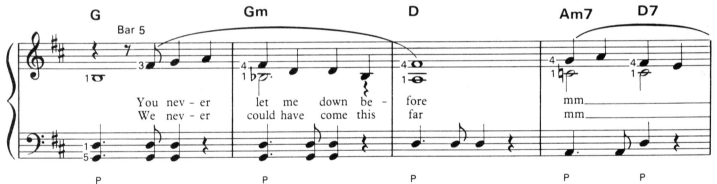

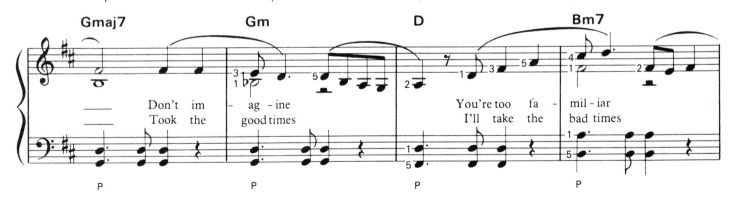

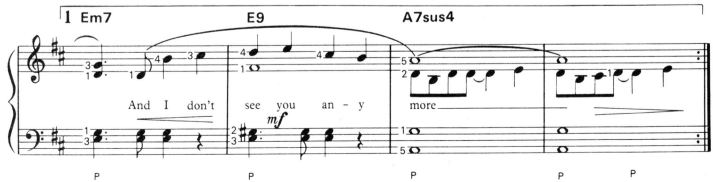

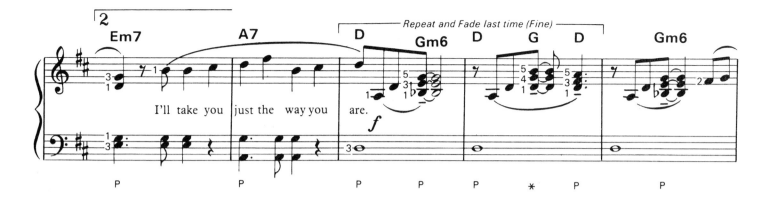

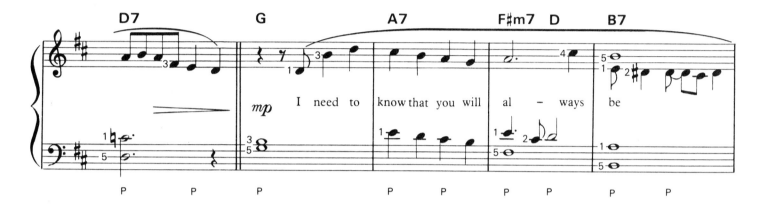

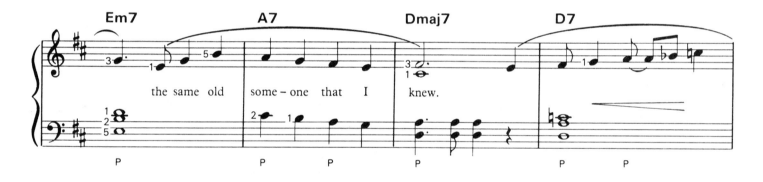

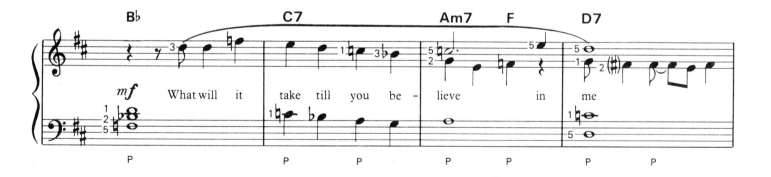

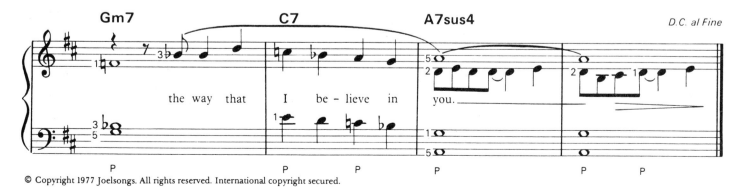

KEY OF G MINOR

15

G Minor is the 'Relative Minor' of B flat
Major, both keys requiring two flats:
B flat and E flat:

Scale/Key of B♭ (Major)

The accidentals likely to occur in the Key
of G Minor are: F♯ and E♮

Scale/Key of G Minor

The following piece begins in the key of
G Minor and modulates (i.e. changes key)
in the last section to B♭ Major.

(THEME FROM) SYMPHONY NO. 40

By W.A. Mozart

Allegro moderato (Moderately fast) ♩ = 92

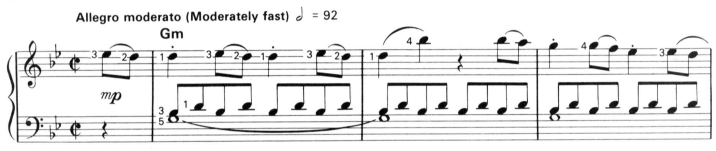

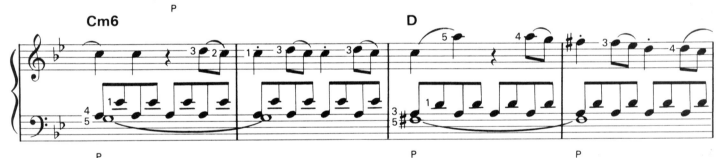

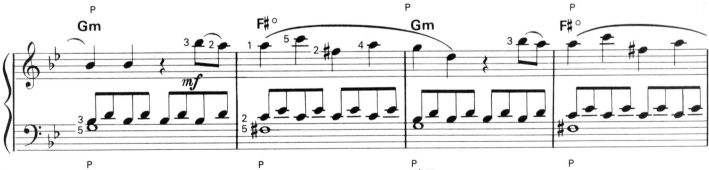

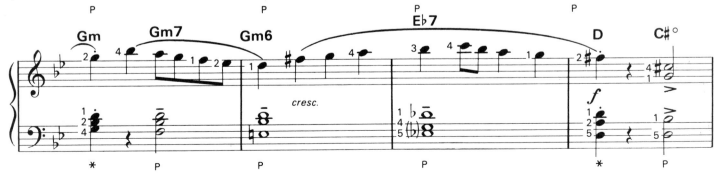

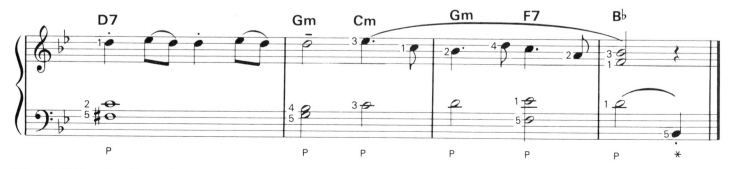

LAST WORD

Congratulations on reaching the end of Book Four of 'The Complete Piano Player'.

In Book Five You will be:
- Playing in $\frac{12}{8}$ time
- Playing in more new keys
- Adding left hand octaves
- Improving your phrasing
- Learning exciting new modern styles.

Till then your last song in this book is:

THANK YOU FOR THE MUSIC

Words & Music: Benny Andersson & Bjorn Ulvaeus

THE COMPLETE PIANO PLAYER
BOOK 5

'By the end of this book you will
be playing with new power and confidence,
and you will be playing 20 popular songs,
including: *Song For Guy, Can't Smile Without You,
The Entertainer,* and *The Theme from E.T.*'

Kenneth Baker

Kenneth Baker

Amsco Publications
New York/London/Sydney

Exclusive Distributors:
Music Sales Corporation
257 Park Avenue South, New York, NY 10010, USA

This book Copyright © 1984 and 1985 by
Amsco Publications
Order No. AM 39645
International Standard Book Number: 0.8256.2439.8

Designed by Howard Brown
Photography by Peter Wood
Arranged by Kenneth Baker

Printed in the United States of America by
Vicks Lithograph and Printing Corporation

CONTENTS

ABOUT THIS BOOK

In this book you will be introduced to many new skills and techniques, which will take you further along the path to becoming a complete piano player. At the same time, the skills you have already acquired from the first four books will be reinforced.

You will learn more about phrasing, and how **dynamics** in music can transform your playing to a remarkable degree. Four new keys are introduced and you will make the acquaintance of $\frac{12}{8}$, $\frac{3}{8}$, and the rare, but interesting, $\frac{3}{2}$ time. New left hand techniques are dealt with; in fact, your left hand, generally, will be strengthened through being able to handle jumps, wide broken chords and octave playing.

As usual, all lessons in this book are based on some of the most popular songs ever written, as well as on famous light classical pieces. In all you will add twenty outstanding new songs to your ever growing repertoire.

WRIST STACCATO AGAIN

We begin Book Five with a lively little number called *Dance Little Bird*.

The Chorus of this piece is a further exercise in 'wrist staccato' for the right hand (look again at Book Two, page 44). Let the hand 'bounce' freely from the wrist joint.

DANCE LITTLE BIRD

Words & Music: Werner Thomas & Terry Rendall

With a marked rhythm ♩ = 66

PLAYING IN ¹²⁄₈ TIME

2

When a piece of music has a time signature of ¹²⁄₈ it means that there are twelve eighth notes, or their equivalent, per bar.

As in ⁶⁄₈ Time (see Book Three, page 16), the eighth notes are grouped into 'threes':

Example 1

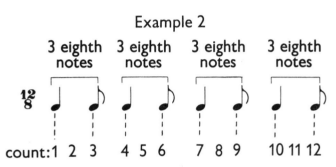

count: 1 2 3 4 5 6 7 8 9 10 11 12

A more typical ¹²⁄₈ bar might look like this:

Example 2

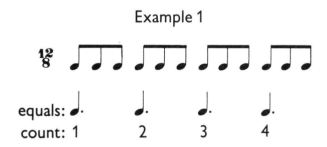

| 3 eighth notes | 3 eighth notes | 3 eighth notes | 3 eighth notes |

count: 1 2 3   4 5 6   7 8 9   10 11 12

Although it is sometimes desirable to count the full twelve eighth notes in a bar (for instance, in the early stages of practice, when you are playing the piece very slowly), it is usually simpler to count four dotted quarter notes in a bar:

Example 1

equals: 𝅘𝅥𝅭   𝅘𝅥𝅭   𝅘𝅥𝅭   𝅘𝅥𝅭

count: 1   2   3   4

Any subdivisions of the beat that occur can be counted as 'a-and':

Example 1

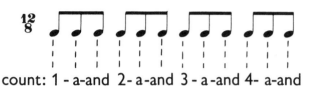

count: 1 - a-and 2- a-and 3 - a-and 4- a-and

Example 2

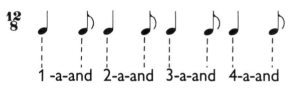

1 -a-and 2-a-and 3-a-and 4-a-and

In Example 1 you play on every beat and every subdivision of the beat; in Example 2 you play on every beat and every 'and' part of the beat. **Remember:** your '1-a-and, 2-a-ands', etc. must be perfectly regular and even, like the ticking of a clock.

With practice you should be able to drop the 'a-and' subdivisions and count only the main beats: '1, 2, 3, 4...'

Your first piece in $\frac{12}{8}$ Time is a traditional American song which has reappeared over the years in various modern arrangements. It's called: *The House Of The Rising Sun.* Here are various ways of 'counting' the melody (which way you choose depends on your stage of practice, and your familiarity with the tune):

THE HOUSE OF THE RISING SUN (Bars 1-4)

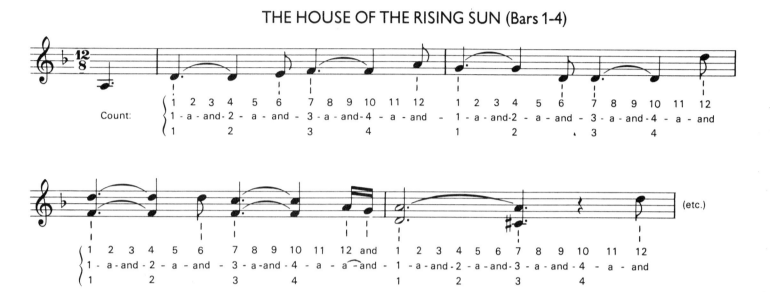

Your second piece in $\frac{12}{8}$ Time is *What A Wonderful World* (page 12). This features a typical modern $\frac{12}{8}$ rhythm pattern in the left hand:

$\frac{12}{8}$

count: 1car-a-van 2 -a-and 3 car-a-van 4 · a-and

Say 'one caravan...' as in normal speech, but be sure to play **only on the syllables shown above.** This should give you the correct sound of this rhythm. Notice that the complete rhythm pattern consists of a 'caravan' group, followed by a simple '2-a-and' group, followed by another 'caravan' group, followed by a simple '4-a-and' group, and so on.

HOUSE OF THE RISING SUN

Traditional

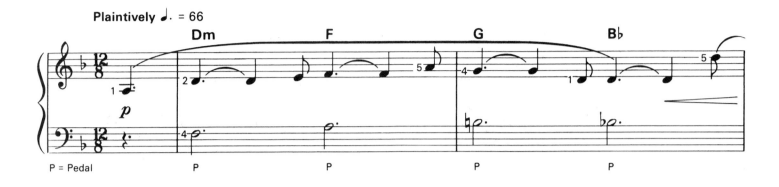

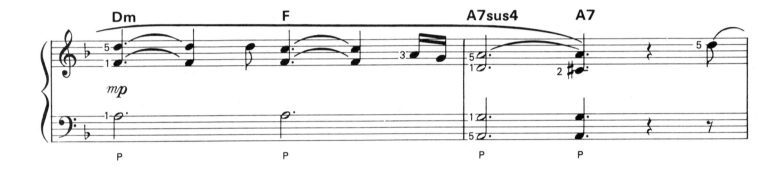

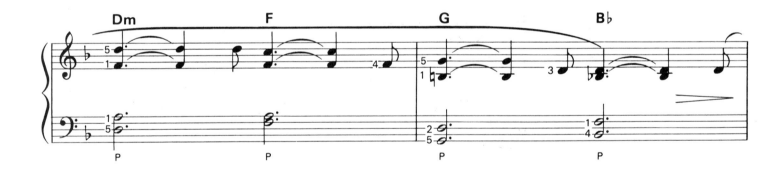

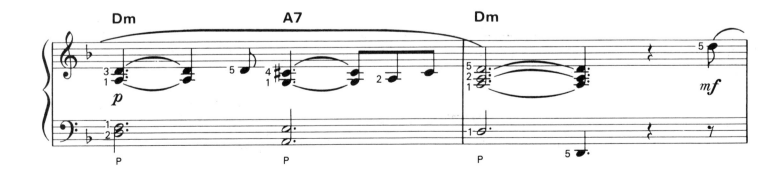

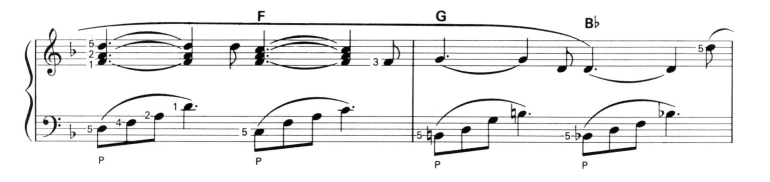

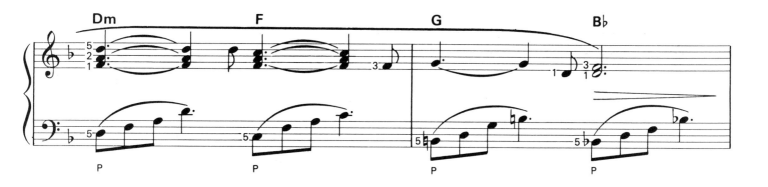

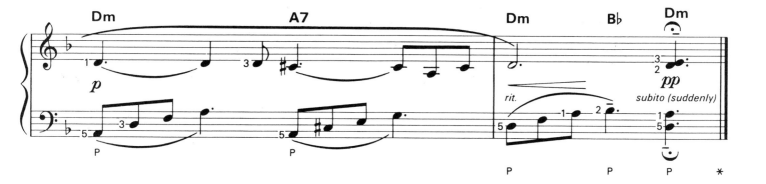

WRIST STACCATO FOR LEFT HAND

3

In the following piece: *What A Wonderful World*, you will be using 'wrist staccato' in your left hand.
Look again at Book Two, page 44. Everything said there about wrist staccato for right hand can be applied equally well to your left hand. Above all don't let your wrist become too tight; let the hand 'bounce' freely from the wrist joint.

Before you play *What A Wonderful World*, turn back to page 9 and read again about the counting of the left hand rhythm patterns in this piece.

WHAT A WONDERFUL WORLD

Words & Music: George David Weiss & Bob Thiele

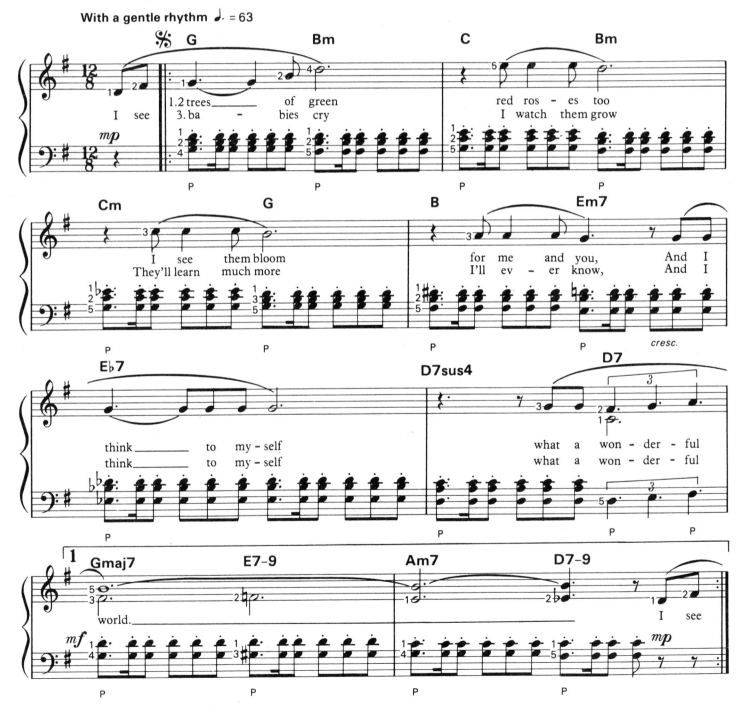

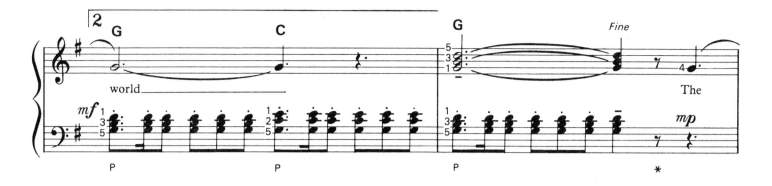

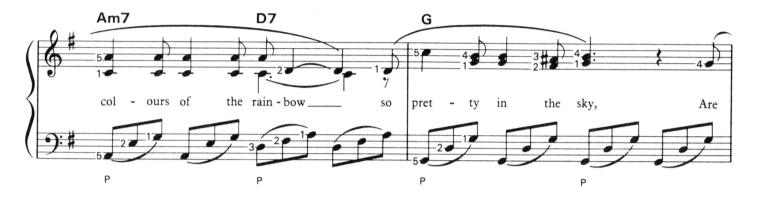

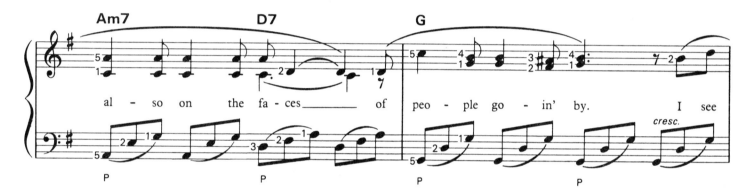

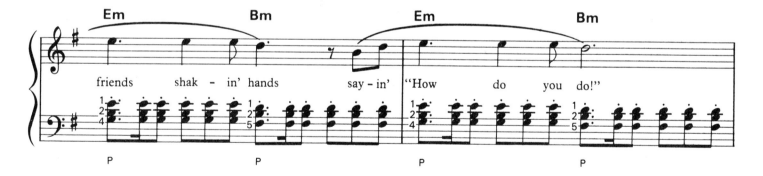

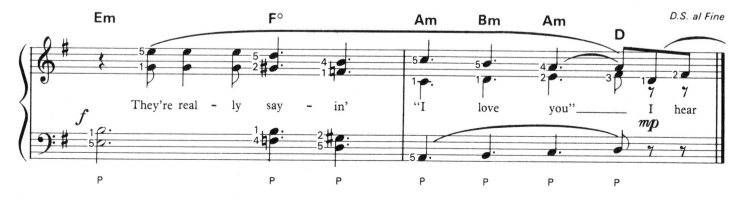

LEFT HAND OCTAVES

4

In the next two pieces: *Swingin' Shepherd Blues,* and *Yesterday,* you will be playing octaves in your left hand. In *Swingin' Shepherd Blues,* for the sake of simplicity, finger all these octaves (including those on black notes) $\frac{1}{5}$.

Before you start to play, practice the scale of C (and any other scales) in left hand octaves, just to get the feel of the distance (see Book Four, page 37–Right Hand Octaves).

In *Swingin' Shepherd Blues* pay particular attention to the 'phrasing' (staccato, accent, and phrase marks). This piece is another good example of 'syncopation' (see Book Four, page 26).

SWINGIN' SHEPHERD BLUES
Words: Rhoda Roberts and Kenny Jacobson. Music: Moe Koffman

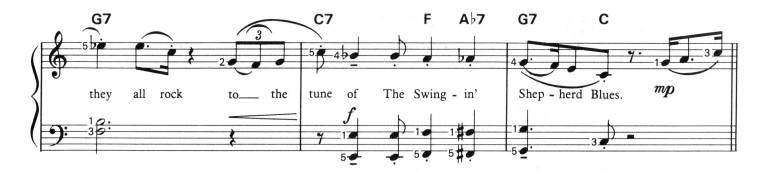

they all rock to___ the tune of The Swing-in' Shep-herd Blues.

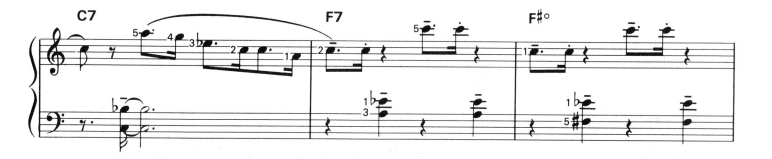

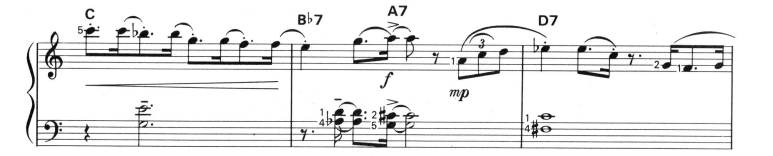

KEY OF E FLAT

5

The Key of E Flat (major) is derived from the Scale of E Flat (major), which requires three black notes: B Flat, E Flat, and A Flat:

Scale of Eb

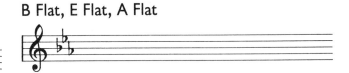

Eb F G Ab Bb C D Eb

Pieces using this scale predominantly are said to be in the 'Key of E Flat'.

The 'Key Signature' for the Key of Eb is:

Key of Eb

B Flat, E Flat, A Flat

When you are in this Key you must remember to play all B's, E's, and A's (wherever they might fall on the keyboard) as B Flats, E Flats, and A Flats.

In *Yesterday* you will be playing left hand octaves more or less throughout. On the white note octaves use fingering $\frac{1}{5}$. On the black note octaves use fingering $\frac{1}{4}$ if this comes easily to you, if not, use $\frac{1}{5}$.

YESTERDAY

Words & Music: John Lennon and Paul McCartney

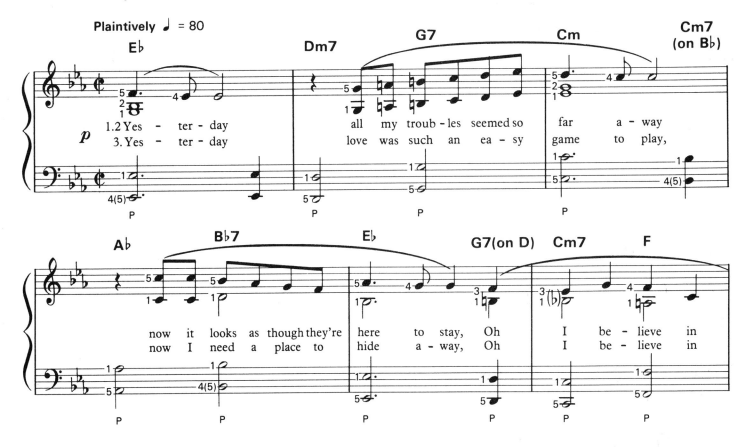

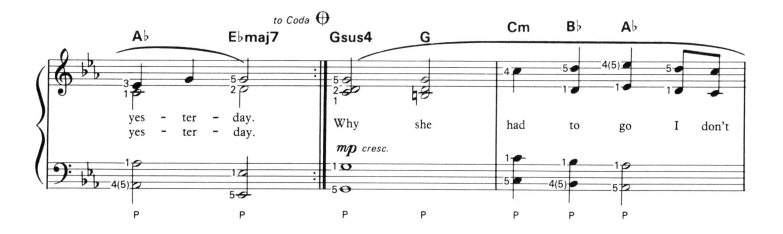

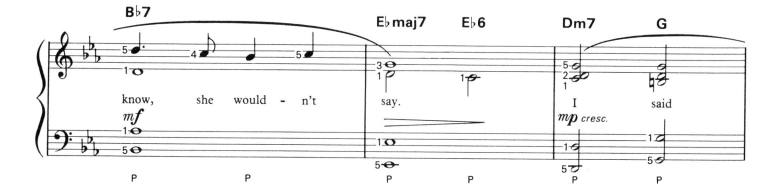

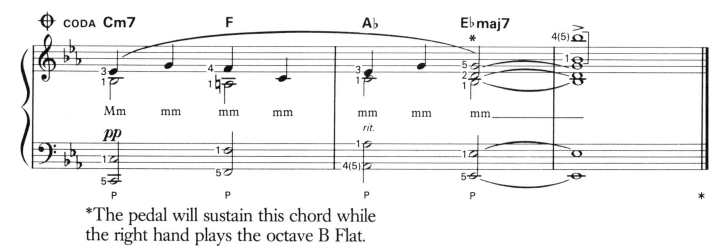

*The pedal will sustain this chord while
the right hand plays the octave B Flat.

DYNAMICS IN MUSIC

6

Dynamics in music are the 'louds', 'softs', 'crescendos', and the like, which help give the music life.

The next piece: *This Nearly Was Mine*, depends heavily for its effect on good dynamics.

Start the piece quietly and calmly. In the middle section (from the Section Lines) play a little louder, then build the tone dramatically, starting with the crescendo in Bar 28.

When you return to the beginning of the piece for the repeat, play boldly and majestically, drawing out the phrases for maximum effect. The climax comes in the Coda, where you must build to a double forte *ff* and make a long, drawn-out 'rallentando' spread over the last three bars.

When played well, *This Nearly Was Mine* is a real show-stopper.

THIS NEARLY WAS MINE
('FROM 'SOUTH PACIFIC')

Words: Oscar Hammerstein II. Music: Richard Rodgers

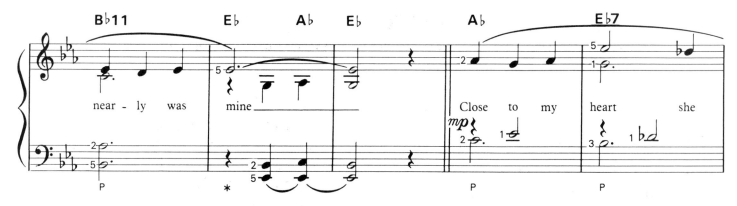

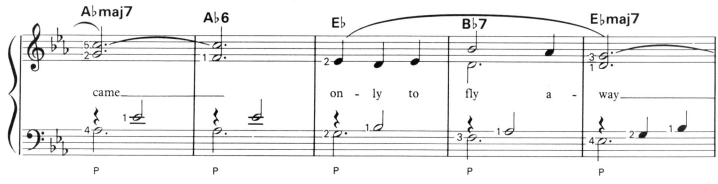

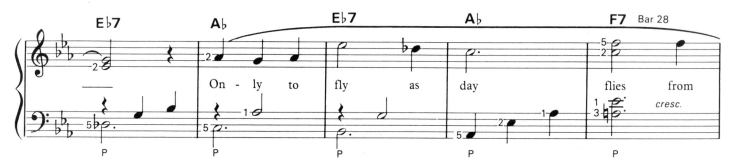

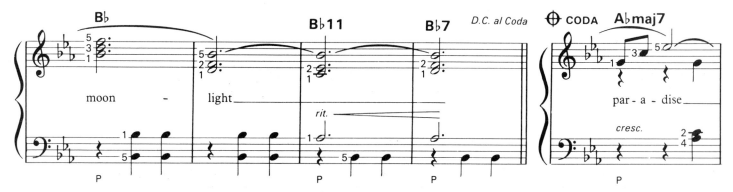

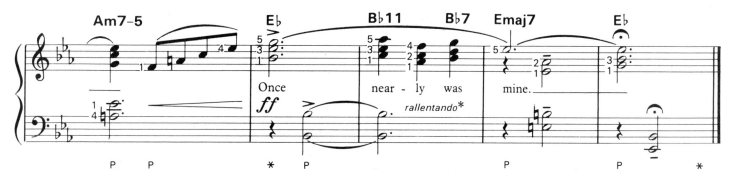

*Rallentando, 'Rall'. for short, means gradually slowing down. A rallentando tends to be more drawn out than a ritenuto.

PHRASING AGAIN

7

Happy Talk is a playful, brash little number, where 'phrasing' is all important.

You will remember from Book Three (page 12) that phrasing is concerned with **how** you play the notes: staccato or legato, with or without an accent, and so on.

See how the right hand double notes in Bars 1 and 2 of *Happy Talk* are to be played 'staccato'. This is so that they will contrast with, and help 'bring out', the left hand melody here.

Note the cross rhythm passages in Bars 7 and 8, and Bars 15 and 16. These will work only if you make the strong accents as marked. This cross rhythm idea continues in the second section (after the Section Lines) in the left hand. Observe all strong accents and staccato markings here.

HAPPY TALK
(FROM 'SOUTH PACIFIC')

Words: Oscar Hammerstein II. Music: Richard Rodgers

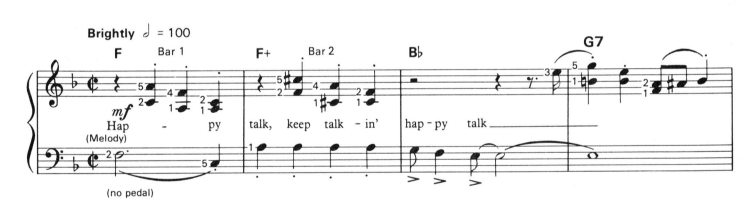

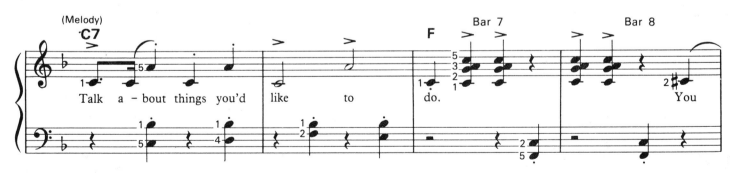

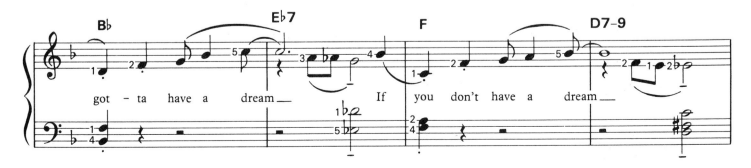

20

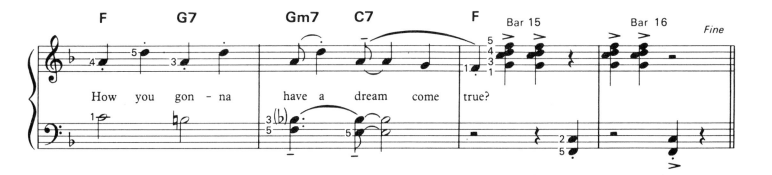

How you gon-na have a dream come true?

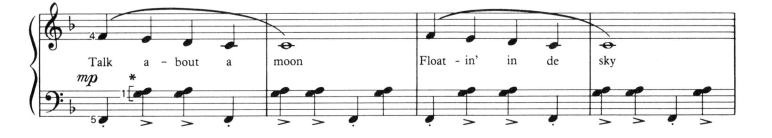

Talk a-bout a moon Float-in' in de sky

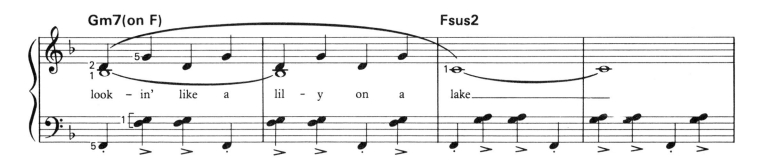

Gm7(on F)   **Fsus2**

look - in' like a lil - y on a lake

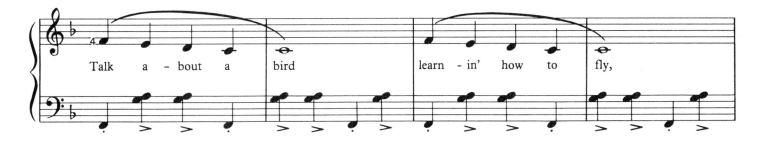

Talk a - bout a bird learn - in' how to fly,

D.C. al Fine

Gm7(on F)   **B7**   **C13**   **C7**

Mak - in' all de mu - sic he can make.

cresc.

*Both notes are played by the thumb.

LEFT HAND JUMPS

8

In the next piece the left hand has to make continuous jumps – down for a low note, up for a chord, and so on. You must develop the capacity to glance quickly down at the keyboard to see where you are going, then back to the music without losing your place.

GYMNOPÉDIE No. 1

By Erik Satie

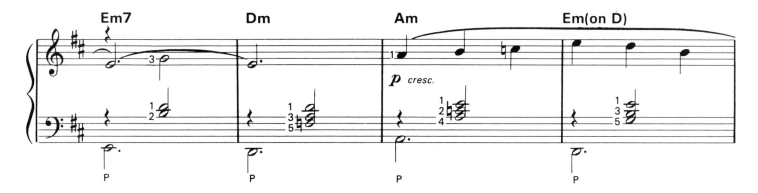

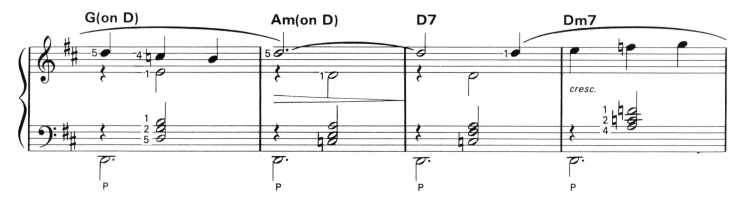

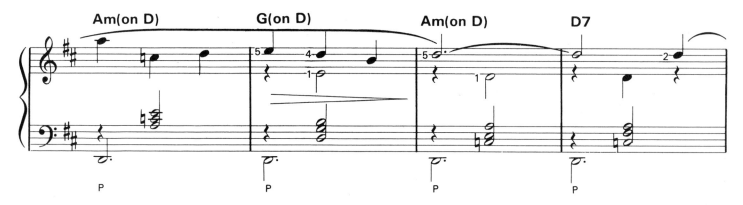

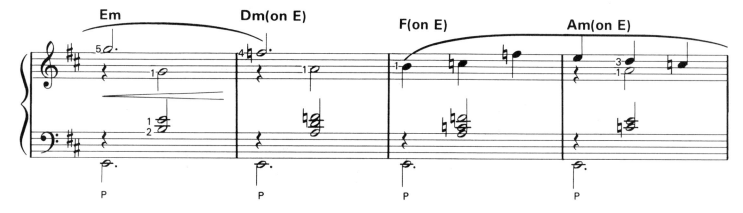

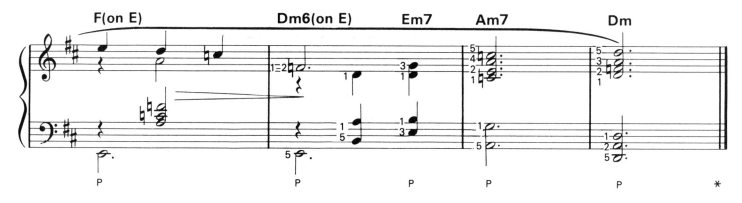

NEW LEFT HAND RHYTHM PATTERN

9

In the first part of *Song For Guy* you will be playing a new left hand rhythm pattern:

count: | 1   2 and 3 4 | (etc)

This is similar to the Bossa Nova rhythm pattern first given in Book Four (page 44):

count: | 1   2 and 3 4 |

The difference in the *Song For Guy* rhythm is that, having played on the 'and' beat, you hold the note down for the rest of the bar.

SONG FOR GUY

By Elton John

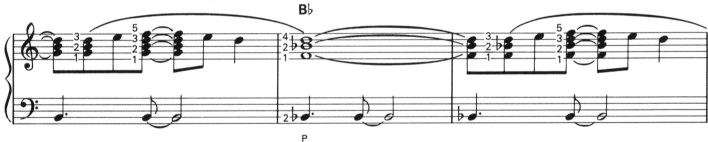

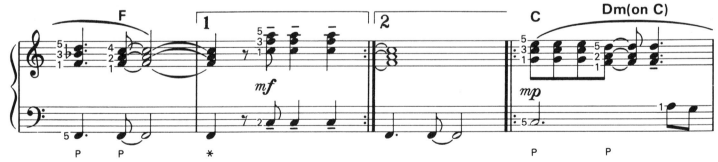

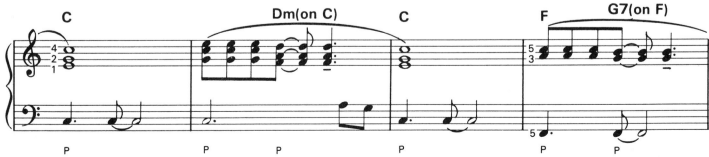

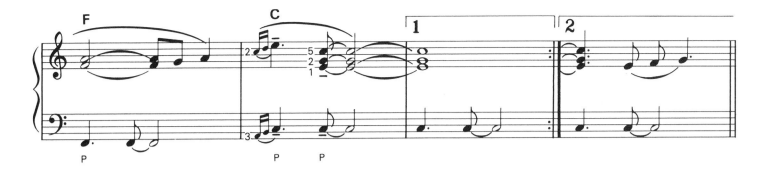

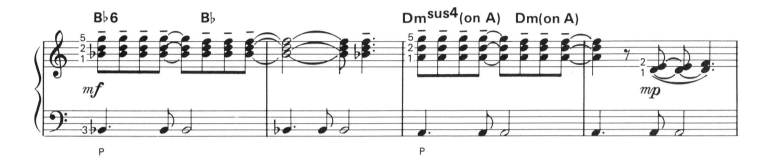

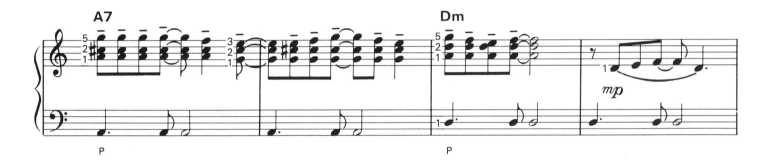

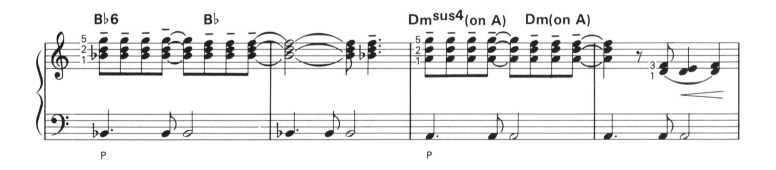

D.C. & Fade on 1st 16 bars

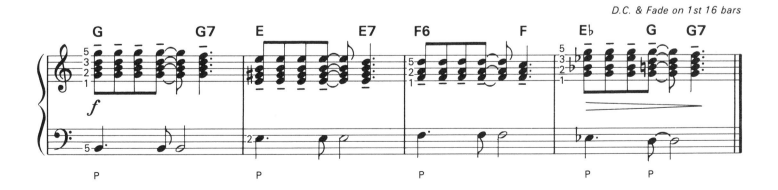

KEY OF C MINOR

10

C Minor is the **relative minor** of 'E Flat Major', both keys requiring three flats: B Flat, E Flat, and A Flat:

The accidentals likely to occur in the Key of C Minor are:

B♮ and A♮

The following piece begins in the Key of C Minor and modulates (i.e. changes Key) at the end to E♭ Major (the **relative major**).

Scale/Key of E♭ (Major)

E♭ F G A♭ B♭ C D E♭

Scale/Key of C Minor

C D E♭ F G A♭ B♭ C

THE SHADOW OF YOUR SMILE

Words: Paul Francis Webster. Music: Johnny Mandel

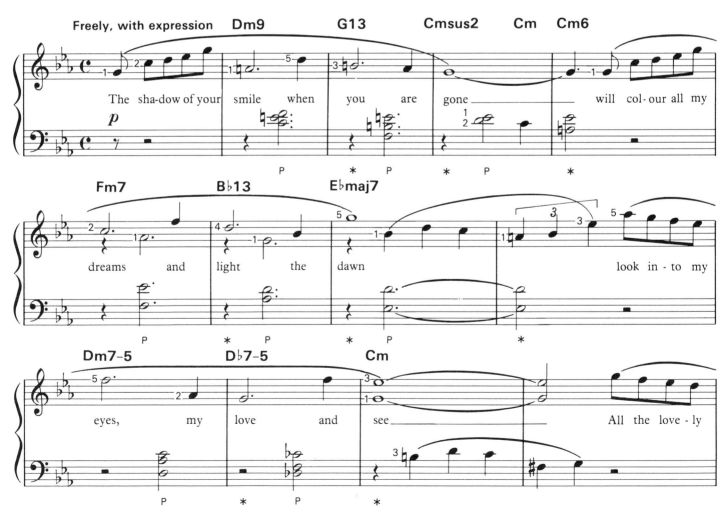

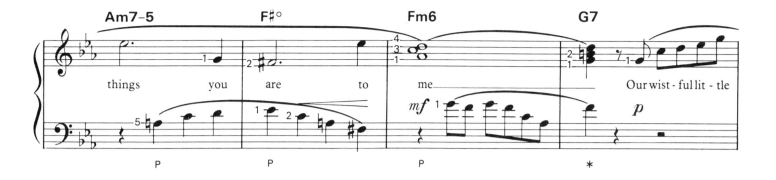

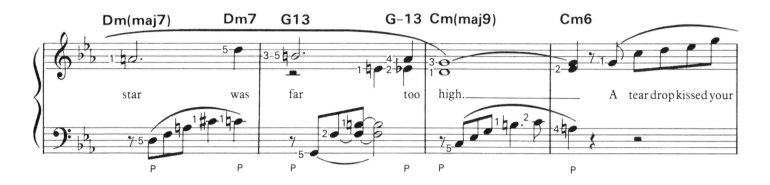

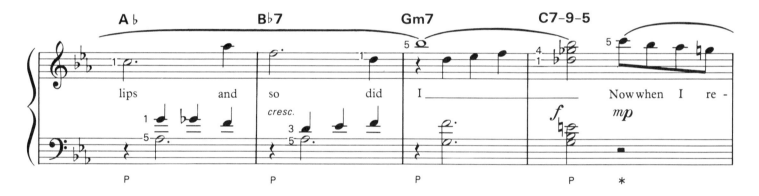

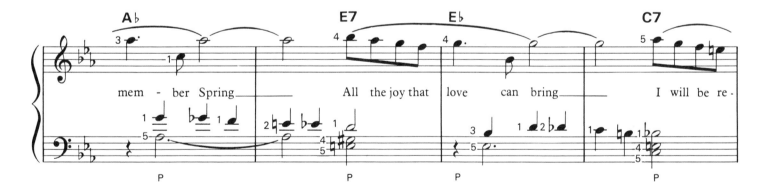

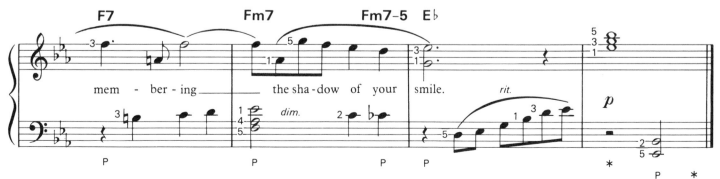

TWO TUNES AT ONCE

In Bars 16-22 of the next piece you play fragments of the main theme of *Can't Smile Without You* with your left hand, while your right hand plays a different theme above it. In other words, you play two tunes at once.

Make your left hand slightly louder than your right hand at this point.

Observe the instruction given at the beginning of the piece: 'with a lilt'.

CAN'T SMILE WITHOUT YOU

Words & Music : Chris Arnold, David Martin & Geoff Morrow

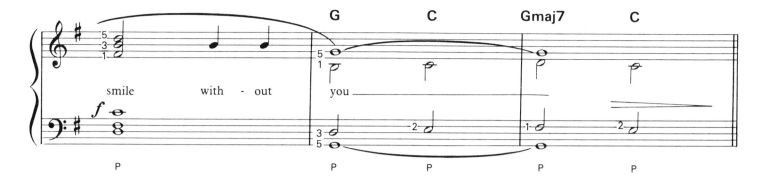

smile with - out you

You came a - long___ just like a song___ Bright - ened my day___

who'd a be - lieved that you were part of a dream Now it all seems___

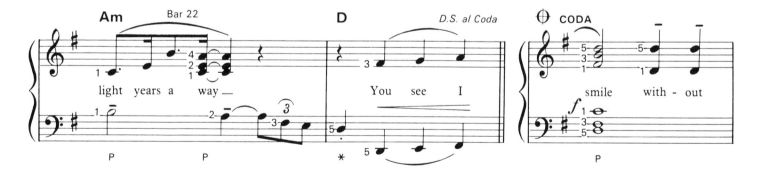

light years a way___ You see I

D.S. al Coda

CODA

smile with - out

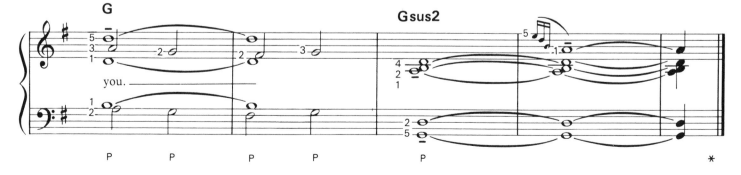

you.___

Gsus2

KEY OF A

12

The Key of A (Major) is derived from the Scale of A (Major), which requires three black notes: F Sharp, C Sharp, and G Sharp:

Scale of A

A   B   (C♯)   D   E   (F♯)   (G♯)   A

Pieces using this scale predominantly are said to be in the Key of A.

The Key Signature for the key of A is:

Key of A

F sharp, C sharp, G sharp

When you are in this key you must remember to play all F's, C's, and G's (wherever they might fall on the keyboard) as F Sharps, C Sharps, and G Sharps.

SCALE OF A

13

Before you begin *Prelude in A Major*, by Chopin, play through the Scale of A a few times with your right hand. This is to help you feel the 'shape' of the key. Here's the fingering for two octaves:

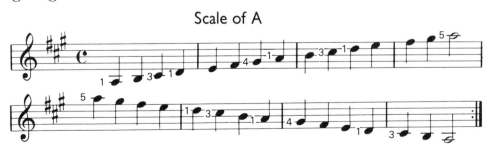

Scale of A

Notice that your thumb plays every 'A' and every 'D', except for the top 'A', which is played by your little finger (5), for convenience.

It is always useful to play through the scale of a new key, since it helps teach the fingers where the necessary black notes lie.

PRELUDE IN A MAJOR

By Frederik Chopin

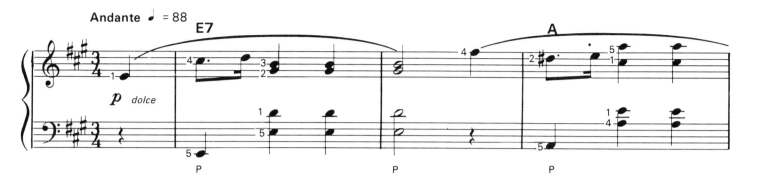

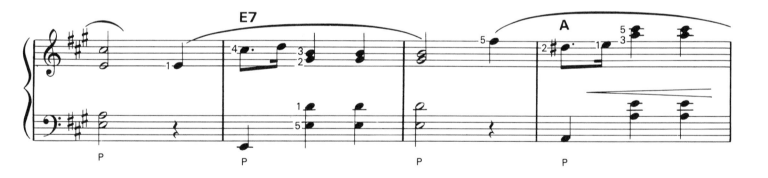

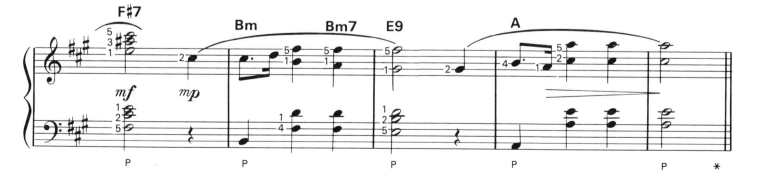

KEY OF A MINOR

14

A Minor is the 'relative minor' key of C Major, in which there are no sharps or flats:

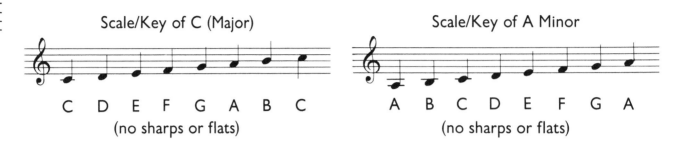

Scale/Key of C (Major)

C D E F G A B C
(no sharps or flats)

Scale/Key of A Minor

A B C D E F G A
(no sharps or flats)

There are two 'accidental' sharps likely to occur in the Key of A Minor. They are:

G♯ and F♯

As it happens, in *Für Elise* (your piece in the Key of A Minor), there is another accidental which keeps appearing:

D♯

This is simply a 'passing note' (see Book Two, page 24), and has no connection with the Scale of A Minor.

⅜ TIME

15

Your next piece, Beethoven's *Für Elise*, is written in ⅜ Time. This means that there are three 'eighth' notes, or their equivalent, to the bar:

Example

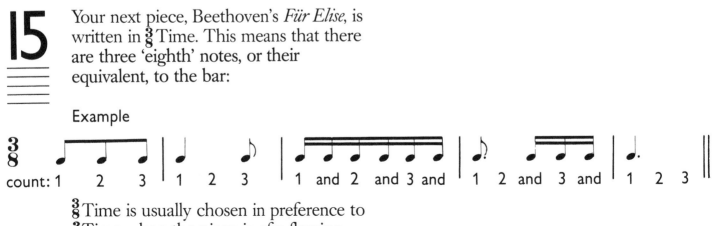

count: 1   2   3 | 1   2   3 | 1 and 2 and 3 and | 1 2 and 3 and | 1   2   3

⅜ Time is usually chosen in preference to ¾ Time when the piece is of a flowing, running nature, like *Für Elise*.

FÜR ELISE

By: Ludwig Van Beethoven

Poco moto (a little motion — quite fast) ♪ =132

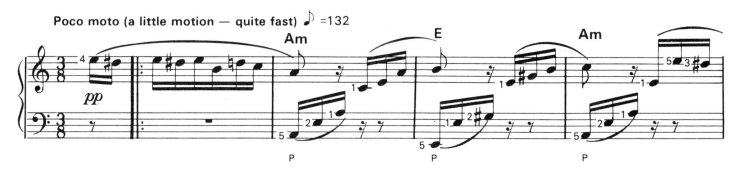

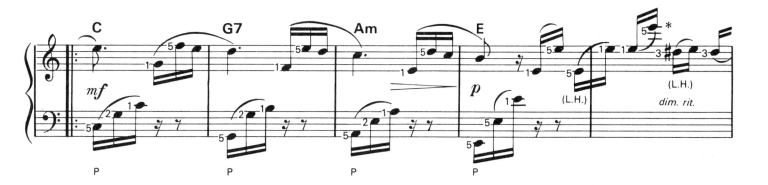

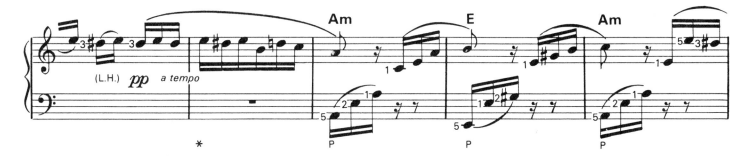

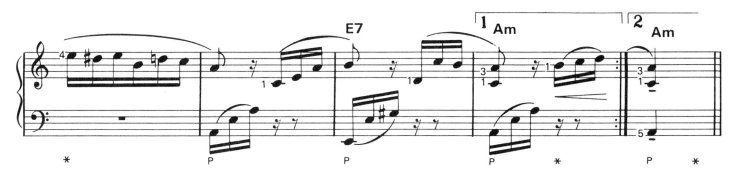

*High E (see p.36)

A STUDY IN ACCIDENTALS

16

Your next piece, *What Are You Doing The Rest Of Your Life?*, is in the key of A Minor. The middle section, however, passes through the keys of A Major, G♭ Major, and F Major, returning again to the key of A Minor for a repeat of the main theme.

This mixture of keys is the reason for the many accidentals (sharps, flats, and naturals, not in the key signature) which you will find in this piece.

WHAT ARE YOU DOING THE REST OF YOUR LIFE ?

Words: Alan & Marilyn Bergman. Music: Michel Legrand

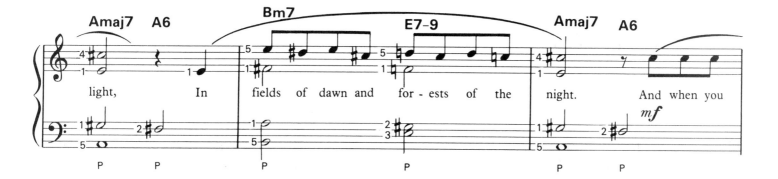

light, In fields of dawn and for-ests of the night. And when you

stand be-fore the can-dles on a cake, Oh, let me be the one to hear the si-lent wish you

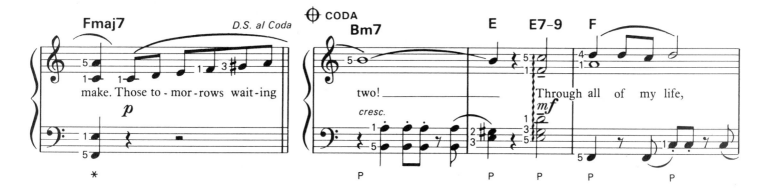

make. Those to-mor-rows wait-ing two! Through all of my life,

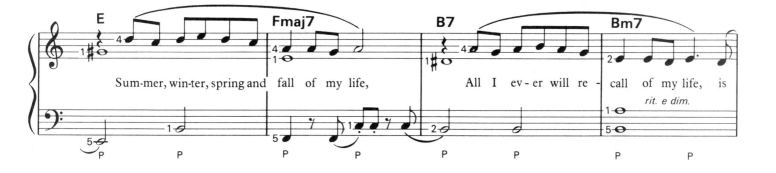

Sum-mer, win-ter, spring and fall of my life, All I ev-er will re-call of my life, is

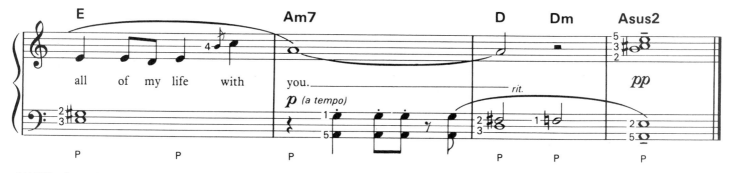

all of my life with you. all of my life with you.

TWO NEW NOTES

High D and E for right hand :

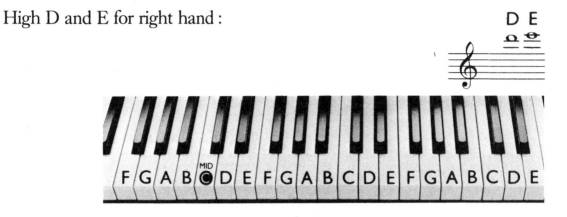

THE ENTERTAINER

By Scott Joplin

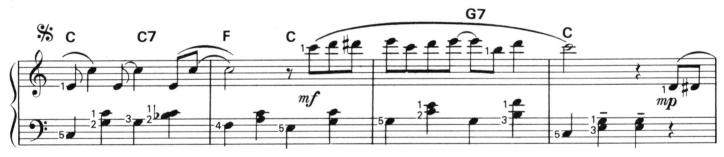

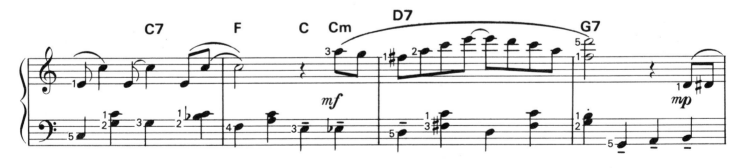

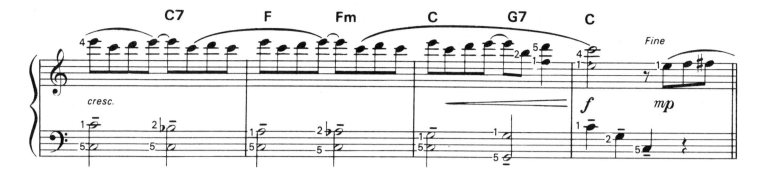

FAST REITERATED NOTES IN THE RIGHT HAND

18

In *With A Little Help From My Friends* there are some fast reiterated 'D's' to be played by your right hand (see Bars 9, 11, and 13).

In such passages it is usual to change the finger on each reiterated note to ensure that the note actually plays again. Here are two exercises for you to practice:

Exercise 1   Exercise 2

Keep very close to the keys.
Observe the accents.
Make sure that all the notes play.
Gradually speed up.

WITH A LITTLE HELP FROM MY FRIENDS

Words & Music: John Lennon and Paul McCartney

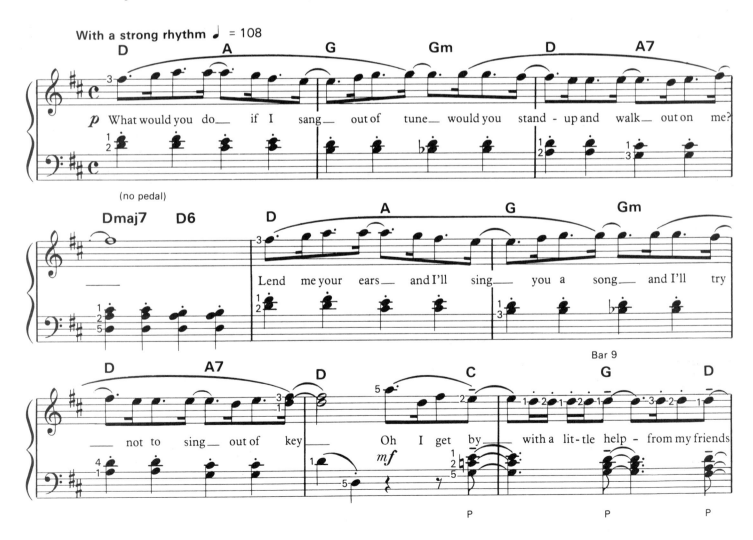

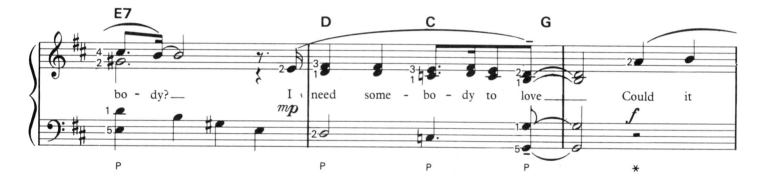

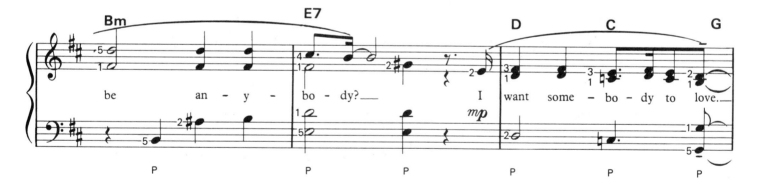

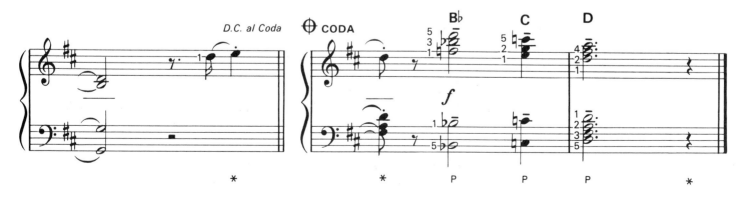

3/2 TIME

19

Your next piece, the *Theme From E.T.*, is written in 3/2 Time. This means that there are three 'half' notes, or their equivalent, to the bar:

Example

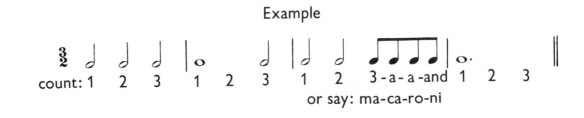

count: 1 2 3 1 2 3 1 2 3-a-a-and 1 2 3

or say: ma-ca-ro-ni

3/2 Time is usually chosen in preference to 3/4 Time when the piece is slow and drawn out, like the *Theme From E.T.*

THEME FROM E.T. (THE EXTRA-TERRESTRIAL)

By John Williams

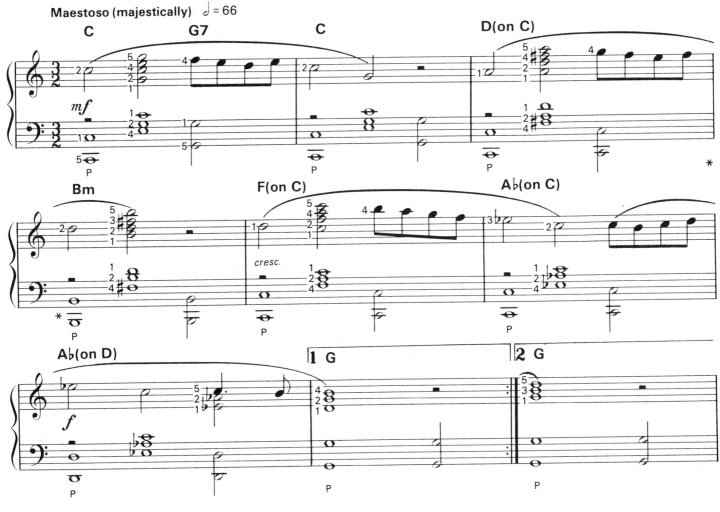

*Low B

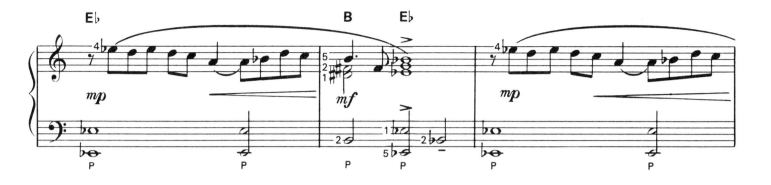

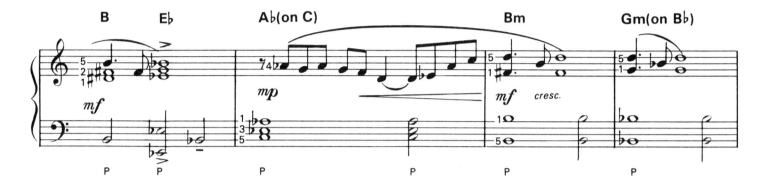

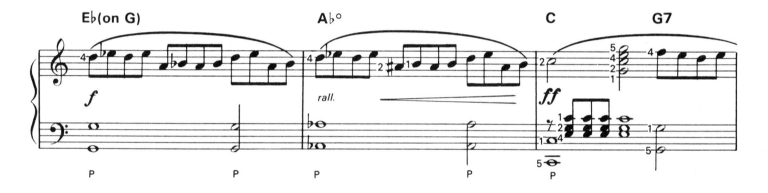

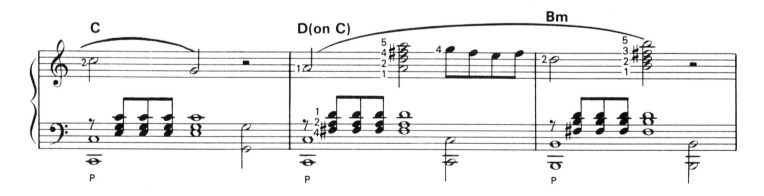

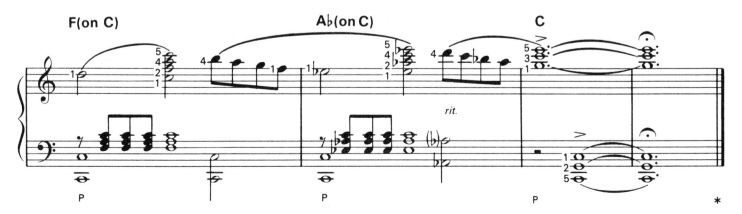

TREMOLO

20 Your next piece: *The Pink Panther Theme*, is an interesting piece of mood music. This comic suspense style theme is greatly enhanced by the use of 'tremolos'.

THE PINK PANTHER THEME

Play the two notes E and B in rapid succession continuously for a bar and a half (six quarter note beats).

Use a rolling action of the wrist on your tremolos rather than finger muscles alone. Do not hold your wrist too tightly.

THE PINK PANTHER THEME
Words & Music: Henry Mancini

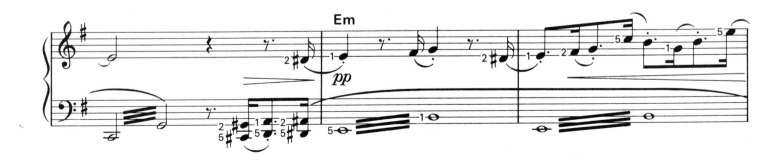

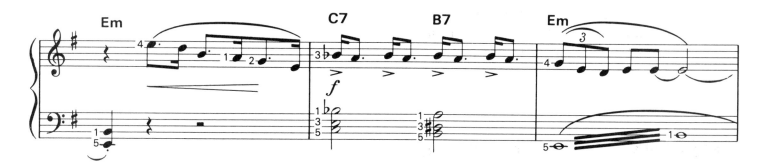

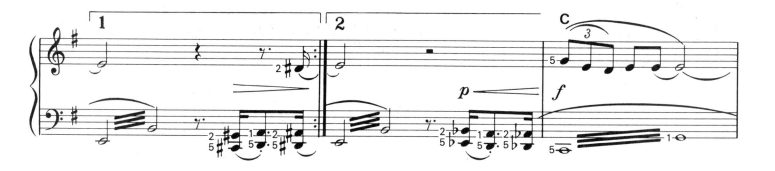

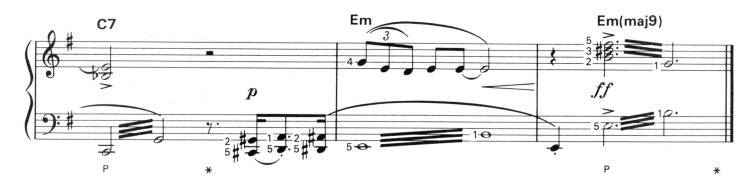

BOTH HANDS HIGH

21 In the next piece, *Music Box Dancer,* both hands play high on the keyboard in order to simulate a musical box. To avoid using a large number of Ledger Lines to express the notes:

- The left hand is written in Treble Clef throughout.

- The right hand is written normally, but is to be played one octave (eight notes) higher than written.
  This is expressed: 8va.

  Try holding down the Soft Pedal (written: una corda) through this piece: it may improve the musical box effect.

MUSIC BOX DANCER
By Frank Mills

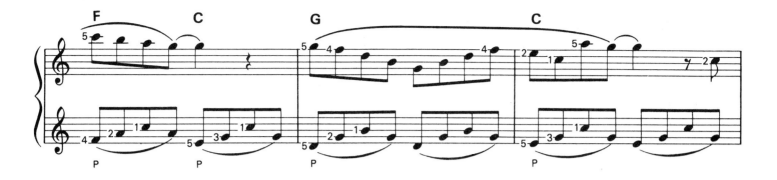

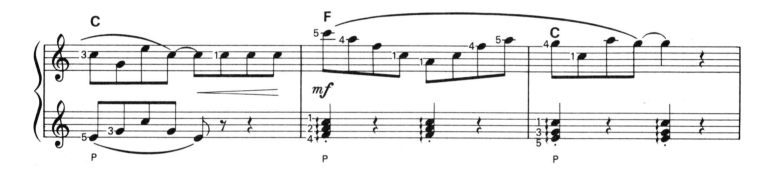

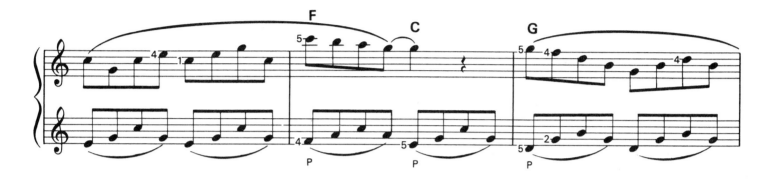

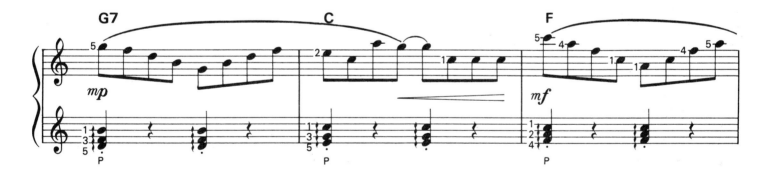

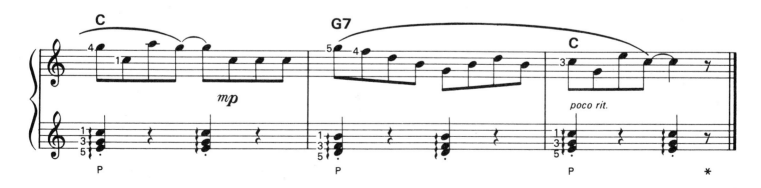

OPEN BROKEN CHORD STYLE FOR LEFT HAND

22 In *Evergreen* your left hand returns again to a 'broken chord' style (see *My Way,* Book Four, page 18, and *Music Box Dancer,* Book Five, page 44). Here in *Evergreen*, however, the chords have been opened up, so the distances you travel will be much greater.

Allow your left wrist to swivel freely from side to side as you encompass the notes.

LAST WORD

So we come to the end of Book Five of 'The Complete Piano Player'. In The Complete Piano Player Style Book you will be studying a number of outstanding piano styles old and new, including: 'Boogie Woogie', 'Blues', 'Shearing Block Chords', 'Country Style', and 'Rock'.

In the meantime here is *Evergreen*:

EVERGREEN
Words: Paul Williams. Music: Barbra Streisand

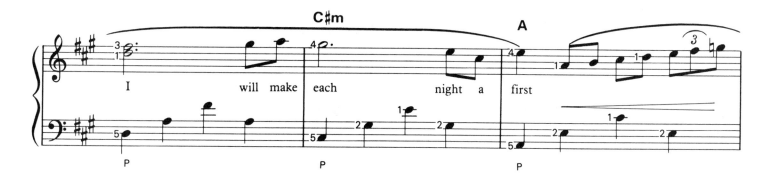

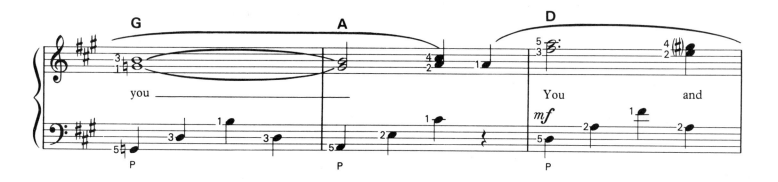

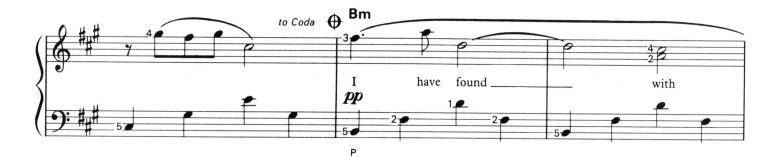

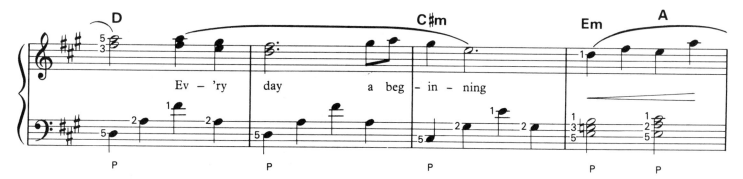

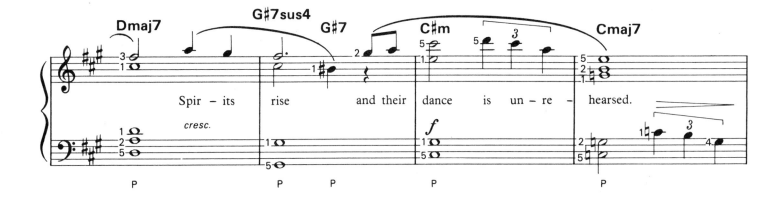

Spir – its   rise   and their   dance   is   un – re – hearsed.

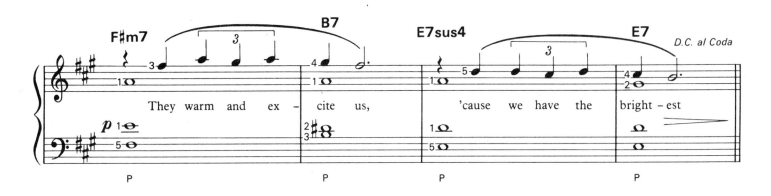

They warm and ex – cite us,   'cause we have the   bright – est

D.C. al Coda

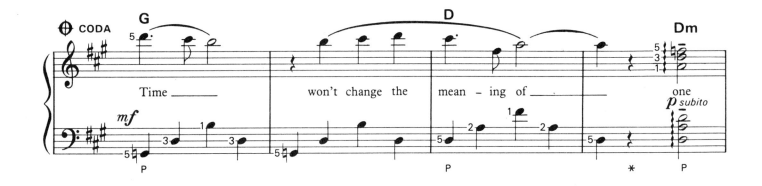

Time _____   won't change the   mean – ing of _____   one

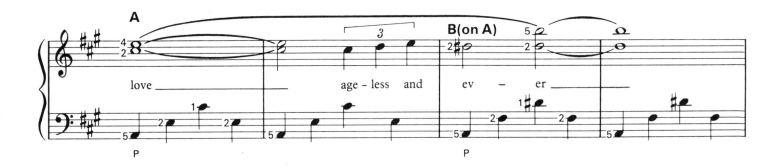

love _____   age – less and   ev – er

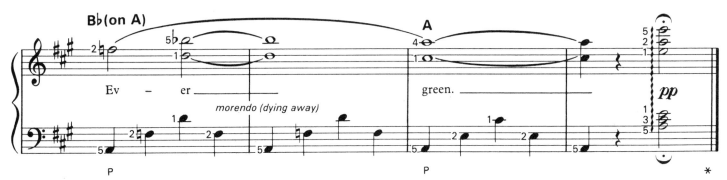

Ev – er _____   green.

morendo (dying away)